KU-079-300

Contents

Dedication

This book is dedicated to my parents Paul and Sheelagh Forrest, who gave me a childhood on an organic dairy farm in Ceredigion, West Wales, which allowed me the freedom to roam and participate in the natural world.

In memory of Pam Fradgley who encouraged me to take on the majority of the throwing at Bronant Pottery, Llandysul, after I had completed my Dip. A.D. at Dyfed College of Art, West Wales.

Miranda Forrest, ceramics in the landscape, 2009. All grogged white stoneware clay. Left: poured glaze in layers: first layer gneiss rock dust, second layer yellow flag iris ash. Centre: poured glaze in layers, first layer cereal straw ash, second layer kelp ash. Right: poured glaze in layers, first layer gneiss rock dust, second layer cereal straw ash. All fired to cone 10 in reduction. Approximately 90 × 24 cm (35 × 9 in.). *Photo: by the author.*

Natural glazes
Collecting and making

Natural glazes
Collecting and making

Miranda Forrest

Bloomsbury Visual Arts
An imprint of Bloomsbury Publishing Plc

BLOOMSBURY
LONDON · OXFORD · NEW YORK · NEW DELHI · SYDNEY

University of Pennsylvania Press · Philadelphia

Bloomsbury Visual Arts
An imprint of Bloomsbury Publishing Plc
50 Bedford Square
London WC1B 3DP
www.bloomsbury.com
BLOOMSBURY and the Diana logo are trademarks of
Bloomsbury Publishing Plc
First published in 2013 by Bloomsbury Publishing Plc
Reprinted by Bloomsbury Visual Arts 2016

ISBN: 978-1-4081-5666-7

Published simultaneously in the USA by
University of Pennsylvania Press
3905 Spruce Street
Philadelphia, PA 19104-4112
www.pennpress.org

ISBN: 978-0-8122-2262-3

Cataloguing-in-Publication Data
CIP Catalogue records for this book are available from the
British Library and the US Library of Congress.

Typeset in 10 on 13pt Rotis Semi Sans
Book design by Susan McIntyre
Cover design by Sutchinda Thompson
Edited by Kate Sherington

Printed and bound in China

738 for

FRONT COVER, TOP: Miranda Forrest, *The Mingulay Bowl,*
2010. Porcelain, fired to cone 9 in reduction, 11 × 27
cm (4½ × 10½ in.). *Photo: by the author.*
FRONT COVER, BOTTOM: All by Miranda Forrest. Left: Wee
dram pot, 2010. Porcelain with glaze from mixed wet
measurements of 1 part gneiss dust, 1 part horsetail
ash. Fired to cone 9 in reduction, 6 x 7 cm (2¼ x 2¾
in.). Centre: Goblet, 2011. Porcellaneous stoneware,
with glaze from mixed wet measurements of 1 part
potash feldspar (purchased), 1 part driftwood ash, 1
part reed ash. Fired to cone 10 in reduction, 7.5 x 7.5
cm (3 x 3 in.). Right: wee dram pot, 2010. Porcelain,
with glaze from mixed wet measurements of 2 parts
gneiss dust, 1 part driftwood ash. Fired to cone 9 in
reduction. 6 x 7 cm (2 ¼ x 2 ¾ in.). *Photo: by the author.*
BACK COVER, TOP: Miranda Forrest, platter (detail).
Porcelain with poured, layered glaze, first layer
gneiss dust, second layer cereal straw ash, third layer
horsetail ash. *Photo: by the author.*
BACK COVER, BELOW: Blue and green tea bowls, 2011.
Porcellaneous stoneware, glazes respectively from
mixed wet measurements of 1 part 'cone 8' base
glaze, 1 part horsetail ash, 1 part thistle ash and 1 part
potash feldspar (purchased), 1 part horsetail ash, 1
part yellow flag iris ash, 1 part cereal straw ash. Fired
to cone 9 and 9+ in reduction, 7 x 8 cm (2¾ x 3¼ in.).
Photo: by the author.
SPINE: Yellow bowl detail, see p. 46.
FRONTISPIECE: Miranda Forrest, bottle, 2002. Stoneware,
peat ash celadon glaze, fired to cone 9 in reduction,
30 × 14 cm (12 × 5½ in.). *Photo: by the author.*
RIGHT: See p. 103.

Acknowledgements

My thanks go to the people of the Uists and in particular of the townships of Bornais and Loch Aineort, who have provided materials and allowed me to collect samples for my experiments, no matter how peculiar my requests may have seemed! Thanks also to Donald Mcleod, the skipper of the boat *Boy James*, who gives me access to the inspiring island of Mingulay, with all its geological features. Also thanks to my partner Graham for not complaining about the multitude of rocks and drying plants that appear in inconvenient places about the house and garden.

With fond memories of the erstwhile ceramics department of The Glasgow School of Art, with its international reputation. I wish to thank the staff for the furtherance of my knowledge and abilities, via the innovative distance-learning ceramics BA (Honours) degree course, and to acknowledge their contributions to the ceramics world at large.

I'd also like to express my gratitude to Alison Stace and Kate Sherington at Bloomsbury Publishing for their editing skills, which have enabled this book to be published.

Miranda Forrest, garden vase with scabious flowers and scabious glaze, 2011. Porcelain, fired to cone 9 in reduction, 7.5 × 5 cm (3 × 2 in.). *Photo: by the author.*

Most of my glazes are made from wild plants (I never think of any of them as weeds!) or farmed crops that I can collect in larger quantities. But it is quite possible to get enough ash for a glaze from garden crops. The scabious flowers in this vase are from perennial plants. I gathered the foliage once it had died back for the winter and turned it into ash, and did the same with the remains of some climbing French beans. This small vase is glazed solely with equal quantities of these ashes.

Bowl, Miranda Forrest, 2011. Porcelain, with glaze from mixed wet measurements of 1 part potash feldspar (purchased), 1 part driftwood ash, 1 part reed ash, 8 × 13 cm (3 × 5½ in.). *Photo: by the author.*

RIGHT: Looking west from the slopes of Beinn Mhor, South Uist, over peat bogs, the 'blacklands' and 'machair' to the Atlantic at Rubha Aird a' Mhuile. The township is Bornais. *Photo: by the author.*

Introduction

When I moved to South Uist in 1999 I felt such a powerful connection to my surroundings that I wanted to bring them literally, as well as metaphorically, into my ceramic work. South Uist is one of the Western Isles of Scotland, also known as the Outer Hebrides, and is composed predominantly of Lewisian gneiss, a 2.9 billion-year-old metamorphic rock.

Initially I was not hopeful of being able to find anything to use. The only natural glaze I knew about was a mixture of clay and wood ash, but South Uist has few trees and I could find no clay. However, after some empirical research and experimentation, I was amazed at the glazes that could be achieved with locally collected materials. Instead of wood as a source for ash, I used herbaceous land plants and marine seaweeds, and replaced clay with other forms of degraded rock. The majority of these made a glaze of some kind. I came to realise that the fundamental principles of making natural glazes were not reliant on finding a specific rock or plant, because several would produce a particular kind of glaze, like a tenmoku or a chun. These glazes originated far across the world from me, in China, where the native materials are superficially different to mine on South Uist, but my results make it apparent that in essence they contain similar minerals. A workable clay body, particularly a high-firing one, may rely on finding a specific kind of deposit, but the choice for glaze materials is far wider.

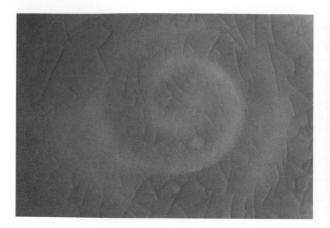 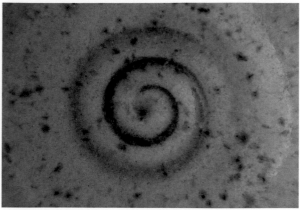

Natural glazes require the sourcing and processing of materials, perhaps in a similar way to when early potters started experimenting to see what would melt when fired. Today, we have the advantage of a scientific knowledge of glaze chemistry that the early potters did not have to inform and direct their search.

Glaze chemistry is a complicated science and much of the knowledge we have about it is industry-led. The ceramics industry has put its resources into the production of highly practical, hygienic and durable glazes. These glazes are made from pure deposits and refined minerals sourced from around the world. Although developed primarily for industrial ceramics, those of us who work in the individual and creative field have nevertheless benefited from and used this technology. The present-day maker can order ready-to-use clay and glaze from a supplier, without any knowledge of the basic ingredients that went into their manufacture. If they wish to give their clay or glaze a more personal resonance, then raw materials can be ordered from the supplier to use in their own recipes. These ingredients, milled to a consistent particle size, arrive conveniently bagged and labelled, ready to weigh out and use. I did just this for a long time, with little idea of what, for example, feldspar looked like in its natural state!

The conventional method of making a base glaze involves complicated formulas and arithmetic. When first in college, I tackled these formulas with interest and gusto, and I well remember the glaze that I produced from long and complicated theoretical study: it was very dry and had nothing to commend it! After that experiment I used a proven base-glaze recipe and adapted it with added ingredients to obtain the colours and textures I wanted. I continued to use these glaze recipes for many years.

When I began using collected materials I had no idea that so many ingredients in my local neighbourhood could be employed to make a glaze. My method of working has evolved from the materials I use and I have accepted that, as I am using natural ingredients, the results may be variable. For the vast majority of my experiments I do not weigh out dry ingredients, but measure them by volume when wet. I use a spoon or ladle to measure and assess the viscosity of the liquid by eye. This has stemmed from firing individual ingredients in the first instance to see what they would do at a given temperature, before proceeding to experiment with layering and mixing.

ABOVE LEFT: Miranda Forrest, bowl (detail), 2011. Porcelain, with glaze from kelp ash and reed ash. Fired to cone 9 in reduction.

ABOVE RIGHT: Miranda Forrest, footed bowl (detail), 2010. Porcelain, with glaze from mixed wet measurements of 1 part 'cone 8' base glaze, 1 part horsetail ash, 1 part cereal straw ash. Fired to cone 9 in reduction.

RIGHT: Miranda Forrest, vase with yarrow flowers, 2011. Stoneware, with glaze from mixed wet measurements of 1 part gneiss rock dust, 1 part horsetail ash. Fired to cone 9 in reduction, 8 × 8 cm (3 × 3 in.).

FAR RIGHT: Miranda Forrest, porcelain bowls, 2010. These bowls show a range of glazes made entirely from materials found within a small distance of my home in the Outer Hebrides. Each bowl: 10 × 20 cm (4 × 8¼ in.). *Photos: by the author.*

Progressing in this way has shown me a wide range of results that can be produced.

I had already begun firing found ingredients singly when I participated in a week's workshop on glazes (purchased materials, not found ones) with the Australian ceramicist Greg Daly. He suggested firing glaze ingredients individually on test tiles, to give an understanding of how they worked; this was a whole new idea for me, and way better than using formulas! I had never thought of firing kaolin or flint individually; as far as I was concerned, they only came as part of a recipe. Daly's way of working with glaze materials influenced me greatly and made me realise that I was better suited to achieving glaze results through working visually (empirically) rather than theoretically (with formulas).

If you prefer the more conventional way of working with dry ingredients, I would nevertheless suggest that you first test your materials wet, as described throughout this book. Find the range of ingredients that give interesting results, at the temperature and in the kiln atmosphere you normally work with, so you know which materials you want to collect in larger amounts. Only then change to using your ingredients dry, as at this stage accurately weighing out ingredients for incremental experiments can point the way to more consistent results.

The sequence of investigation and experimentation in this book follows the natural order of evolution: rocks, vegetation and animal derivatives.

Miranda Forrest, bowl, 2010. The porcelain clay body of this bowl is visible, as the foot does not have any glaze on it. The glaze on the main part of the bowl is a layer of kelp seaweed ash with a layer of cereal straw ash on top, both brushed on. This is an example of a glaze that has little alumina in it. During firing, it has run to form a pool of 'glass' in the centre. Fired to cone 9 in reduction, 10 × 21 cm (4 × 8¼ in.). *Photo: by the author.*

1

What is a ceramic glaze?

The ceramic glaze

It is thought that the origins of adding a glaze to a clay form stemmed from early potters observing deposits of ash leaving shiny areas on their ware when firing to high temperatures with wood. They had the ingenuity to try putting ash on the pots before they were fired, and after that, natural inquisitiveness led them to experiment and see what else would melt to form a glaze.

A contemporary ceramic piece is conventionally made up of a clay body covered with a thin layer of glaze. This covering is generally applied as fine particles, suspended in water, in a separate procedure to the making of the clay body. In the heat of firing these particles melt to form a glaze that fuses with the clay underneath.

A glaze may have varied functions, from the visual one of added interest and decoration, to the tactile one of introducing different textures, or the practical one of forming a smoother and more resilient layer on the outside of the clay wall.

To make your own natural glaze, some understanding of the underlying science is beneficial. A glaze is, in essence, glass, and predominantly made up of silica. Natural silica can be found as quartz, an opaque white crystalline rock. It does not look like clear glass because it has taken thousands of years to slowly cool, allowing the crystals time to grow; if silica is re-melted and then cooled rapidly, it makes a clear glass.

Pure silica only melts at very high temperatures (over 1700°C/3100°F) but combined with a flux (potassium, sodium, calcium, magnesium: individually some of these also have high melting points) the melting point is lower. The temperature at which the combined ingredients melt is called the eutectic. For a glaze on a ceramic piece, this melted mix then needs a stabiliser to stop it flowing off the clay and onto the kiln shelves. This stabiliser comes in the form of alumina (pure alumina melts at over 2000°C/3700°F). By stabilising a glass to make a glaze, alumina also widens the maturing temperature range. The main difference between float glass and glaze is that glass has less alumina in it.

Put simply, to make a glaze you need silica, alumina and a flux. In the right balance and within a certain temperature range they make a stable base glaze to which other ingredients can be added for colour or texture. A stable base glaze will have its own maturing temperature range; take it higher and it will run, fire it lower and it will not melt. The key to firing a ceramic piece is that all the ingredients must mature – that is, produce the effect you want – at your chosen temperature. This includes the clay body.

I generally fire to cone 8 to 10 (1265°C–1300°C/2309°F–2372°F) because this is the highest I want to go and it melts a range of materials. Raising the firing temperature will increase the range of materials that melt. If you fire at lower temperatures, although fewer materials will melt, you may still be surprised by what you can use. Natural iron ochres and clays can be used at temperatures in the region of 1000°C (1832°F).

2

Recognising natural glaze materials

Glaze materials from rocks

In effect, all glaze materials come from the ground – from rock. This is the ceramicist's basic palette of materials, so it helps to have some understanding of what rocks are. I would say at this point that the subject can get very complicated, so I have tried to clarify information and focus on materials that pertain to ceramics. For an overview of this subject, I can recommend reading a basic geology book (see some suggestions in the Bibliography, p. 110).

Approximately 99% of the earth's continental crust is made up (discounting oxygen) of the following eight elements: silicon 62%, aluminium 16%, iron 6.5%, calcium 5.7%, magnesium 3.1%, sodium 3.1%, potassium 2.9% and titanium 0.8%. Under the sea, the percentages differ slightly. These elements are found in glaze materials as:

- **Silica**. Silicon, combined with oxygen to form silica, the glass/glaze maker, is found in abundance.
- **Alumina**. Aluminium, combined with oxygen to form alumina, the glaze stabiliser, is plentiful.
- **Fluxes**. Calcium (whiting/lime), magnesium (talc), sodium (soda) and potassium (potash) are all fluxes.
- Iron and titanium provide colour in glazes.

LEFT: Miranda Forrest, tea bowl, 2011. Porcellaneous stoneware, glazed with brushed layers of ochre, reed/wrack mix and iris (iris only on the inside). Fired to cone 9 in reduction, 9 × 9 cm (3½ × 3½ in.). With sleeping garden tiger moth. The plinth stone is a 2900 million-year-old Lewisian gneiss rock.

RIGHT: Cliff face of Lewisian gneiss with intrusion of white and pink feldspar/quartz rocks.
Photos: by the author.

Varying combinations of these elements are what create the rocks of the land we live on. To simplify how different rocks form, it is predominantly the rate of cooling of magma that determines how minerals and oxides separate out and crystallise into various rock varieties. The earth's molten magma contains considerable quantities of iron. When this magma cools relatively quickly, it is likely to become an iron-rich basalt-type rock, typical of the seabed. Alternatively, if the magma remains below the surface and spends some 10,000 years slowly cooling, crystals will begin growing when it reaches the region of 1200°C (2192°F). The first crystals to form, at the highest temperatures, are the heavier metal ones like olivine and pyroxene, which contain a lot of iron. Because these crystals are heavier than the remaining magma they can drop or otherwise separate from it. This changes the composition of the magma to a purer, lighter (andesitic) magma. This magma in turn can continue to grow crystals to become granites, feldspars or quartz when solid. Feldspar and quartz magma is the lightest, with the least iron, and can rise or otherwise seep upwards through cracks in cooler rock until it too solidifies to form seams, sills and dykes. These incursions vary in size and small seams can often be seen in exposed rock faces (p. 15). The amount of iron remaining in granite-type rocks is variable, but much less than in basalt types.

The permutations of pressures, temperatures and cooling times mean that the combinations of minerals that make up the rocks in the earth's crust are innumerable. Because of this, rocks are often named after the period when they solidified or metamorphosed (re-formed under pressure and/or heat, but did not re-melt) rather than the often numerous minerals they are made up of. So rock names are frequently not helpful to anyone looking for glaze materials, as the names do not always correlate with those of the ceramic materials we use.

Benbecula, Outer Hebrides. The pink rock in the foreground is pegmatite feldspar; behind it, a darker, iron-rich rock can be seen. *Photo: by the author.*

After rocks have spent thousands of years solidifying and coming to the surface of the planet, they then commence the long process of decomposing by erosion through weathering. This leads to deposits of particles of similar size and weight, transported by air or water, for example, clay, iron ochre or sandstone. Alternatively, deposits can be the remains of a rock after some of its minerals have leached away. Kaolin (china clay) and white porcelain-type clays originate from decomposed feldspars where the flux component (potash, soda, lime) has washed away, leaving the silica and alumina behind.

Some understanding of geology and mineralogy will give you a greater breadth of knowledge in the fundamentals of ceramics. In my case, it has added to my enjoyment of the whole experience of collecting raw materials and made me appreciate the age of the materials I work with; it emphasises the connection between the earth we live on and the ceramicist's art. But it isn't necessary to have a deep geological understanding of the region you work in to be able to make a glaze. Some geographical knowledge of your locality is enough to find raw materials for experiments.

I have found that, in the field, a general idea of which minerals are present in a rock or deposit is all that can be expected. Unless you can do a scientific analysis of a material, which is rather unrealistic for small samples, how it melts in the kiln at a given temperature will more readily provide the information a ceramicist needs at a practical level. Rocks and deposits can be broadly grouped into those that are iron-rich, basalt-type and fire dark, the feldspar/quartz that fire white, and the granites that have a small amount of iron in them and fire somewhere in between (see p. 18).

Rocks at the edge of a beach. The softer degraded rock is eroding more quickly than the harder seams embedded in it. *Photo: by the author.*

Specific rock groups and derivatives

Iron-rich rocks

In practice, this group contains any rock that has cooled without discarding iron from the magma plus separated iron-rich crystals such as olivine or pyroxene. As silica, alumina and fluxes are present, iron-rich rocks and crystals often melt at stoneware temperatures. They can form an excellent base for dark glazes. The rocks to look for are any that are dark, but contrarily iron can be present even when the rock does not look dark.

Over time – and this could be a long time – these rocks can decompose to produce a range of deposits, sediments, clays, subsoils and iron ochres. They can be found in places where they are exposed, either by natural erosion or by human excavation. Naturally eroded cliff faces of all sizes can be found anywhere, from mountainous regions through to seashores. Watercourses, whether large rivers, gorges or small streams, uncover materials and produce natural deposits. Pebbles on the beaches often come from different rock types, as can be seen with the naked eye, but using a magnifying glass will give more information on any fine crystalline structure.

Rocks are quarried all over the world on a large or small scale, and such quarries are a good source of fine rock dust. Quarries extract either a specific rock type or a mixed rock used for general aggregate purposes. Rock dust is produced by stonemasons, and the debris from borehole drillings may be fine enough to use in a glaze.

It is worth investigating any excavations for building foundations, as rocks, subsoils or clays may be exposed.

From left: dark, iron-rich, fine-crystal, basalt-type rock; white feldspar/quartz-type rock with little or no iron in it; the next two and the big rock behind are all granite-type rocks with varying amounts of iron. *Photo: by the author.*

A feldspar outcrop.
Photo: by the author.

Feldspars and granites

Conventionally, alumina has always been introduced into a glaze in the form of one of the feldspars (ground into powder form) rather than as pure alumina. Combined in the feldspar mineral are all three of the ingredients that we are looking for to make a glaze: silica, alumina and flux – usually potash or soda, but also lime (calcium). This means that feldspars fired as a single sample often melt at stoneware temperatures and give an uncoloured result.

Feldspar is a mineral that will either form a rock on its own or be found combined with other crystals in a rock. The rock known as granite is mainly made up of fused crystals of feldspar, quartz (silica) and mica. The commonly used ceramic material Cornish stone is a granite with very little iron it. Nepheline syenite is a high-alumina feldspar. Feldspars and low-iron granites provide silica, alumina and flux in varying amounts and have traditionally been the prime ingredient of conventional stoneware-glaze recipes.

Feldspar rock varies from white to pink in colour and has a shiny, cleaved surface. The pink (though it can also be white) is typically potash feldspar, also referred to as pegmatite (large crystal form) or orthoclase (alkali). White is typically soda (albite) or lime/calcium (anorthite) feldspar, also referred to as plagioclase.

Naturally occurring granites vary in content and need to be fired to find melt and colour results.

Depending on your location, feldspars and granites are not hard to find. In the field it is difficult to know what variety of feldspar you have found, and even to be sure it is not quartz. You are looking for any rock that is white, pink or even yellowish, often in the form of seams in other rocks. Fire a fragment to see how it behaves and use it accordingly. Feldspar has a characteristic sheen on the cleaved surface that is unlike the crystal structure of pure quartz. Feldspar rocks weather more freely in hot climates and can be found decomposing in many parts of the world, becoming kaolin in places where the flux element has leached away.

Look for these materials in the same places as the iron-rich ones described on p. 18. Use a magnifying lens for a closer look at different rock crystals.

Silica-rich rocks

Because silica makes up nearly two-thirds of the earth's crust, it is abundant in rocks combined with other minerals, and so is present in the ones discussed already. On its own it forms quartz crystals and flint pebbles. A high percentage of sandstone is actually silica sand re-formed into a rock.

Quartz can be identified as a white crystalline rock, noticeable as seams running through darker rocks and as fine crystals in granite rocks. Quartz is a hard mineral, harder than feldspar. This can be used as a guide to differentiate them. The theory is that quartz scratches glass easily and feldspar scratches it with difficulty!

Flint (silica) nodules are found in chalk deposits, identifiable as pale cream, hard, knobbly pebbles. Sandstone quarries are possible sources of silica-rich rock dust.

Deposits

Sand

Quartz crystals are very hard and they fracture, retaining a crystal shape while other minerals grind to a dust. Pure silica-sand deposits have long been quarried worldwide for the glass industry. Sand on the beach can be small particles of rock from varying sources such as silica crystals, any other local rock particles and seashell particles. Examining a sample through a magnifying lens helps identify different types of grains. Fire a small sample (in a saucer to protect kiln shelves) to see if it melts.

Clay, slate and shale

Clay is widespread around the world in one form or another, ranging from pure kaolin consisting entirely of silica and alumina to deposits with a high percentage of iron and other impurities in them. Local knowledge is the first line of enquiry as to whether there is, or has ever been, a brickworks or clay quarry nearby. In areas where the garden soil is a clay type, it is worth investigating the subsoil. Also, investigate streams, riverbanks and sea cliffs for clay (see pp. 73–5).

Shale is a sedimentary rock originating from compressed clay or mud deposits. Slate is the same as shale but has also undergone metamorphism.

Water-course deposits

Fine particles found on the edges of rivers, lochs or lakes are most likely to be particles originating from rocks nearby, but they could also have been transported some distance along watercourses. They will have similar attributes to the parent rock but can have the advantage of needing little or no grinding.

Subsoil

Subsoil is any material below the high-organic-matter soil present in the top layer. Depending on geological and weathering events it can consist of any rock type.

Iron ochre flowing down rocks and into the sea. Mingulay Bay, Outer Hebrides. *Photo: by the author.*

Iron ochre

Iron ochre is a naturally occurring iron pigment that probably contains a small amount of clay/other rock particles. It can be found in places oozing out of cracks in rocks and in slow-moving watercourses. In this state it is often fairly fluid, and the colour varies from yellow through to a dark red-brown but is best characterised as 'rusty'. Iron ochre is surprisingly abundant and can often be spotted by an observant walker.

Peat is cut for fuel in many parts of the world and the resultant ash is not usually wanted. Peat is the compressed remains of sedges or mosses and so derived from plants. The ash I have tested is predominantly from moss peat and the result is high in iron with little silica or flux apparent. I suspect this iron originated from a fluid iron ochre that suffused the peat during its formation.

Pan iron is a deposit of waterborne iron ochre that has percolated downwards and settled where it has met a barrier. It can be so hard that something metal, like a knife, is needed to collect it. It is most easily found where it has been exposed – for example, at the eroding edge of beaches.

Metal compounds

It is worth enquiring locally as to whether any metal ores such as copper or manganese are known of in the vicinity. If there have been mines in the past, there may still be small quantities worth finding. Firing samples should give an indication of any oxides present. I have found iron in abundance and some evidence of titanium in my local gneiss rocks.

Glaze materials from plants

Plants require minerals, which they find and take up through their roots. Plants with different structures require different minerals: a tree will not have the same requirements as a grass. As with rocks, an exact analysis of these materials is not necessary to develop a glaze. The general guidelines for plants grouped according to a particular dominant mineral, as described in this section, must be regarded as just that. A test firing will tell you how your local plant ashes behave.

Silica-rich plants

Plants use silica for strength in their stems, and some plants' ashes contain a much higher ratio of silica to flux. This becomes apparent when a test sample is fired. If a plant ash is very high in silica, it will remain a powder when fired, even to cone 10.

The plants to look for that are likely to be high in silica are often those that grow quite tall for their size. The poaceae family (formerly gramineae) includes rice, reed and any cereal crop grown for human or animal consumption, as well as the grass that grows on your front lawn. Common reed occurs throughout the world's tropical and temperate zones and is often used for thatching. Rice is widely cultivated for human consumption, especially in Asia. Cereal crops are cultivated for food in large parts of the world and include such crops as wheat, oat and maize. These plants are grown for seed but, once harvested, the rest of the plant is a by-product that can be used as a glaze material.

Wood ashes from different tree genera will vary in the amount of silica they contain. The percentage is generally higher in tropical zones than in temperate ones.

Alumina

I have found that results from experiments using a single plant ash tend to give either an unmelted powder or a runny glaze. Even combined plant ashes do not produce what I regard as a balanced glaze. Plants seem to contain inadequate levels of alumina for controlling a runny glaze, so a rock source is usually required.

Fluxes from plants

When the early potters fired with wood and found that fly ash left a glaze on the shoulders of their pots, what was happening? Wood ash, high in flux (calcium) was combining with the silica and alumina on the clay and forming a glaze. High-flux ash glazes can be recognised by a typically 'stringy' or runny look. Although this is a known wood-ash effect, many plant ashes will provide varying amounts of flux for natural glazes, and those from marine flora have particularly aggressive fluxes in the form of sodium and potassium salts.

This makes the list of plants to look for rather long. Herbaceous plants are often easier than trees to experiment with as they can be collected and processed in smaller amounts. Keep in mind the different groups or families of plants. Trees and grasses have already been mentioned. Some other suggestions are flowerless plants, such as ferns, bracken, horsetails, mosses and seaweeds. These reproduce by spreading spores and occur worldwide. The flowering plants are made up of numerous families, all of which can be experimented with. Examples are plants of the apiaceae family (formerly umbelliferae) such as parsley or angelica; the iris family; urticaceae, including stinging nettle; and the polygonaceae family, which includes dock and knotweed. All the various families grow worldwide. What matters initially is that you source plants that are easy to collect and process. It is likely that if you test a range of different plant varieties in your locality, you will find glaze results along the same lines I have.

As well as the colloquial name, the table shown opposite gives the family name of the plants tested. This allows them to be identified internationally. It is a guide to inform the sourcing of plants native to your locality. Tree families are too numerous to mention.

Family name (Colloquial name of test example)	Results alone at Cone 8	Comments	Family range
Apiaceae, formerly umbelliferae (wild angelica)	Dry glaze	Mixes well*, some blue	North America / Eurasia
Fabaceae, formerly leguminosae (bean plants)	Melts	Mixes*	Worldwide
Dennstaedtiaceae, formerly hypolepidaceae (bracken)	Melts	Results better when mixed*	Worldwide
Poaceae, formerly gramineae (cereal straw)	Dry pale glaze	Excellent layered or mixed*	Worldwide
Poaceae, formerly gramineae (common reed)	Remains a powder	Needs a strong flux	Tropical and temperate ones
Polygonaceae, or buckwheat (dock, broad-leaved)	Pale brown, melts	Mixes well*, some blue	Temperate zones
Athyriaceae (lady fern)	Melts	No colour	Worldwide
Gramineae (grass)	Remains a powder	Needs a strong flux	Worldwide
Equisetaceae (horsetail)	Melts	Excellent layered or mixed*	North America / Eurasia
Iridaceae (iris, yellow flag)	Melts and runs	Excellent layered or mixed*	North America / Eurasia
Polygonaceae (Japanese knotweed)	Melts and runs	Excellent layered or mixed*	Temperate zones
Urticaceae (nettle)	Melts	Good layered or mixed*, green	Eurasia / North America
Typhaceae (reed mace/cattail)	Melts	Shows promise (only small sample)	Northern temperate zones
Juncaceae (rush)	Dry	Only small sample	Temperate zones
Laminariaceae (seaweed, kelp)	Pools, crazes, 'glass'	Potent flux	Worldwide
Fucaceae (seaweed, wrack)	Several varieties tried, all melt	Mixes well*, strong flux	Worldwide
Asteraceae: formerly compositae (thistle)	Dry	Mixes well*	Worldwide
Onagraceae (willowherb)	Melts	Shows promise (only small sample)	Temperate zones
Wood (mixed ash)	Melts and runs	Excellent layered or mixed*	Worldwide

* = mixed with other materials

Marine plants: sources of flux

There are large 'forests' of kelp in the sea in many parts of the world. The individual plant stands more than a metre (40 in.) high on strong thick stipes (stems) with strap-like fronds at the top. Storms can wash large quantities of broken-off stipes onto beaches. The wrack seaweed plant is noticeably different to kelp; the stipe is much smaller and the 'leaves' form a much larger percentage of the plant by comparison. This family includes bladderwrack (*Fucus vesiculosus*), commonly found growing attached to rocks, midway between high and low tidelines.

All seaweed tested gave a melted result, indicating they contain flux, probably in the form of potassium or sodium salts. Although kelp and wrack seaweeds were identified and continued with in my experiments, I also found other unidentified seaweeds gave a similar result, so any convenient ones are worth testing.

LEFT: This horsetail grows to about 30 cm (12 in.) high. It is a member of the equisetaceae family that can be found in America, Europe and Asia.

BELOW LEFT: Common reed, a member of the poaceae (formerly gramineae) family.

BELOW: Two plants that provide glaze materials growing in my 'garden': flowering wild angelica and yellow flag iris leaves. *Photos: by the author.*

Flat wrack (*Fucus spiralis*) growing anchored to a feldspar/quartz pebble, surrounded by darker iron-rich rocks. *Photo: by the author.*

Glaze materials from animals

Eggshells, seashells, corals and bones are a source of calcium and can be used as a flux.

A more commonly used calcium flux comes in the form of chalk, known in ceramics as whiting, which is rich in calcium carbonate. This soft rock is compiled from the remains of invertebrates that collected over millennia at the bottom of large bodies of water. These remains then became compressed into vast sheets. If they are metamorphosed, they become the harder rock known as marble. Chalk rocks often have flint nodules embedded in them.

Chalk can look similar to kaolin in the raw state: both can be found as creamy white deposits of considerable size. However, chalk lacks the sticky, plastic properties of clay that characterise kaolin. Some chalk deposits can have varying amounts of iron in them.

Gypsum

Gypsum, mined in many places, is the common name for calcium sulphate and is used to make plaster of Paris. In rock form it is also known as alabaster. It is incompatible as a glaze material. If a small amount of 'plaster' is incorporated in a ceramic piece, it will 'explode off' during firing and leave a crater.

Newly-burnt yellow flag iris
leaves. This plant makes a fine
ash that is easily sieved.
Photo: by the author

3 Preparation of materials

Processing materials from rocks

Equipment

When starting to experiment with natural glazes it is sensible to use only small amounts of materials, to avoid wasting time processing large quantities. Little extra equipment is needed beyond what the average working ceramic studio holds. As work progresses and materials are required in larger amounts, a jar or ball mill will make processing easier and faster. A ball mill is a receptacle that rotates slowly to grind particles to a smaller size. To aid grinding, it contains porcelain balls of varying sizes, along with water and the material to be ground. Any material that can be ground to a powder in a pestle and mortar will grind well in a ball mill, but this device will not crush hard rock.

Processing hard rocks

I have classified as a 'hard rock' any rock or pebble in its natural state that is too hard to grind by hand with a pestle and mortar. These can probably be broken up with a lump hammer into small fragments but will not grind to a dust. Feldspar, quartz and

A selection of equipment used for sieving and grinding. Jugs are useful and plastic containers with lids are needed. Silicon spatulas are good for collecting materials from the bottoms of buckets. *Photo: by the author.*

FAR LEFT: Unfired rocks in the kiln. They had some shells put in with them before firing (just after the photo was taken).

LEFT: The rocks are in the same basic positions after firing. This photograph of the fired rocks shows the colour change that some rocks undergo and the one rock that shattered. Fired glaze results from these samples can be seen on p. 57. *Photo: by the author.*

most granites fall into this category. However, if they can be heated to red-hot for a few hours, once they have cooled it is quite possible to break them up and grind them. I advise caution when heating rock. Some rocks and pebbles will explode when heated; flint pebbles (quartz) are prone to sudden, violent shattering as the temperature rises. I was told by one artist that he had destroyed a kiln when rocks exploded as they were being heated!

I have done no experiments on a large scale, but I do put small rocks into the bottom of the kiln when biscuit firing, the rocks measuring no more than 6 cm (2½ in.) in any direction. Some shatter as the temperature rises, so to protect the kiln and any clay ware from damage, soft firebricks are used to wall off the rocks, with an old kiln shelf underneath and another as a cover on top. The kiln also has a flue to take away any possible fumes. A biscuit firing reaches 1000°C (1832°F) on the pyrometer but it is probably cooler at the bottom of the kiln. Michael Cardew, in his book *Pioneer Pottery*, recommends that rocks are not heated to more than 950°C (1742°F), though he does not explain why.

I suggest using some kind of referencing system if you are heating more than one rock sample. 'Before and after' photographs, like the ones shown above, will help, as some rocks change colour a surprising amount.

Processing degraded rock or rock dusts

By sieving

Assuming that the degraded rock or rock dust has particles in it that are fine enough to go through at least a 60-mesh sieve, test a small sample to ascertain whether it is worth separating out a larger amount. Sieve with enough water to separate the smaller particles from the unwanted bigger ones.

To process a larger amount of dust or degraded rock, collect it in a standard 15l (32 US pints) bucket and add enough water to cover it. Into a separate bucket containing 10l (21 US pints) of water, immerse the mesh of a domestic sieve, containing a third of the sieve's volume of rock dust, and agitate it freely. Throw out the particles that do not go through the sieve and repeat the process until the required amount is done. Then re-sieve with a finer mesh. A brush will help move the particles through the sieve during this laborious stage. Keep the sieve mesh just below the water surface. The finer the particles, the better they will adhere to the biscuit-fired clay surface, but sieving through a 60-mesh will suffice.

With a ball mill

If you have a ball mill, experiment to see if the particles will grind in a pestle and mortar; if they do, they will also grind in a ball mill. It will depend on the sample whether or not any preparatory sieving is required.

Processing ochres and clays

Iron ochres generally require little water to sieve them, just enough to sieve out any debris. Pan iron that is hard may need light grinding before sieving. Clays need thorough wetting, and perhaps should be left to soak, so that they turn into a slip before sieving.

A small jar or ball mill.
Photo: by the author.

Processing wet sediments

Sediments are often fine particles that need no grinding. However, they can sometimes have a pungent odour that comes from incorporated rotting vegetation! If this is the case, sieve and dry samples for storage. If kept in the wet state, for obvious reasons it is advisable not to keep sediment in an enclosed container in a warm environment!

Processing plants

Please read Chapter 12, Health and safety, with particular regard to burning marine plants (p. 107).

Collecting, drying and burning

All land and marine vegetation needs to be converted to ash for use as a glaze material. 1 to 2kg (2 to 4lb) of vegetation is enough to gather for initial experiments.

Seaweeds can be collected at any time of year. Those that have broken off from their anchors and washed up on beaches are more pleasant to handle and process when fresh. It seems to make little difference to the end result what time of year land plants are harvested, but it can make a big difference to the ease of processing. Stems are generally much easier to collect and dry when they have died back, rather than when they are green. This is usually in autumn and winter, but varies for different plants.

Plants need to be thoroughly dry before they are burnt. Grass lawn cuttings are rather hard to dry, as they are cut while green and lush and a pile gets compacted easily; it will need regular turning. Do not add any easily combustible material to

Kelp stipes (stems) laid over raised wood supports so that the airflow is unimpeded. Drying stipes this way takes some time and depends on the weather. Completely dry stipes will re-absorb moisture. Wrack seaweeds are comparatively easier to dry than kelp. *Photo: by the author.*

ABOVE LEFT: Various metal trays for burning small quantities of materials and an old washing-machine drum for larger amounts.

ABOVE RIGHT: A purchased brazier. Braziers and other metal containers tend to rust if left outside and need cleaning with a wire brush before use, to avoid contamination from iron oxide. *Photos: by the author.*

'get the fire going', as this will contaminate the ashes. For vegetation that is initially difficult to light, like seaweed, a gas flame from a portable burner can be used; once lit, dry plant material should burn without further assistance. **Be aware that some dry plants burn surprisingly fiercely. Do not inhale the smoke.**

Burn material outside on a non-contaminating surface that facilitates the collection of the cold ash. On a windless day, small amounts can be burnt on a metal tray.

For larger quantities, a brazier may be needed. Any metal container with a base to catch the ash, large enough to hold a sufficient quantity of material to keep the fire burning well and with holes low on the sides to allow in air, will make an excellent brazier. Metal buckets or dustbins with holes punched in the sides can be tried, and a recycled washing-machine drum works well for me, but metal bins with a flue in the lid are also available. Wind direction and strength need to be taken into account, as fine particles can blow away while burning, and these are what you are trying to collect!

Ashes

Allow ashes to cool before disturbing them. Many plants produce very fine ashes that easily blow away. Ashes left outside to cool, unprotected from the elements, can disappear in a breeze or get washed away by rain. A brazier gives some protection from wind and a metal sheet over the top will shield the ashes from an unexpected shower.

Ashes are not a benign material to handle. Wet ash slops are caustic to the skin, so wear waterproof gloves when handling any ash, whether wet or dry. Dry ash becomes very easily airborne and thus inhaled, so always wear an adequate mask when disturbing dry ashes.

At this stage a decision needs to be made as to whether the ashes will be stored wet or dry, and whether they are going to be washed. I use all ashes in a wet state as I find them more pleasant to work with. One of the reasons for washing them is that high levels of salts in ashes can be carried into the clay wall and cause damage during firing. I have found this a particular problem with marine ashes (see p. 48). However, washing out water-soluble salts also means losing a lot of the ashes' fluxing ability. I start by doing tests with unwashed ashes, only washing them if there is a problem. As yet I have not found it necessary to wash land vegetation ashes, although many people who work with wood ash always wash it. If unwashed, deflocculating of the glaze slops can also be a problem (see p. 67). In the end, whether to wash ashes or not will become a matter of personal preference.

Processing unwashed, but wet, land ashes

If you are planning to retain salts, use as little water as possible. For ashes that are going to be used unwashed and wet, carefully scoop them when cold directly into a small amount of water. The amount of water needed can be very deceptive and it is less than might be thought, judging by the volume of ash! Start with a small amount of water, about a sixth of the volume of ash, then add more as needed. I use a spatula to gently push the ash down into the water, which breaks down the ash structure and enables me to judge the amount of water needed. Aim for damp rather than wet at this stage.

The next step is to put the ash through a domestic sieve. Recycle the sieved liquid to control the quantity of water used. You are aiming for a liquid the consistency of single cream that suspends the ash particles and yet is capable of being poured or brushed onto a biscuit-fired surface.

Sieving through a domestic sieve is all that is necessary for most land vegetation ash for a first test firing. A 60- or 100-mesh sieve will give a finer particle size, as will ball milling for an hour or so.

Processing ashes for accurate dry weighing

If a clean sample of land vegetation is well-burnt, it will give a pure ash that can be accurately weighed, and this should be stored in an airtight container for later use. If there is debris in the ash, as is often the case with wood ash, this will affect accurate weighing. Unless a way of calculating the weight of the debris can be found, it will need to be sieved out. Dry sieving tends to make ash airborne, while wet requires it to be dried out afterwards by evaporation, in order to retain water-soluble salts.

Processing marine ashes

Marine vegetation ashes are very caustic. The ash may need grinding before it will go through a sieve. When using a pestle and mortar, have the ashes damp, but not wet enough to splash. An hour or so in a ball mill will make sieving easy. Any requisite washing should be done after grinding.

Sieving reed ash through
a domestic sieve.
Photo: by the author.

Washing ashes

To wash any variety of ashes, add a generous amount of water, stir them well, then allow the particles to settle before discarding the water. It is optional whether or not you should wash the ash a second time, but it is usual to do so. It is easier to sieve ashes with more water, so combine this stage with washing. If washed ashes are to be dried, the process can be speeded up by putting them in porous biscuit-fired bowls kept for this purpose.

Processing materials from animals

Eggshells, seashells and bones will all provide the flux calcium. 'Roasting' them will make grinding easier. When calcium has been heated it becomes quicklime (calcium oxide), which is caustic to skin. When slaked with water it is reputed to 'spit' but I have not found this with seashells. Seashells grind easily after they have been roasted in a biscuit firing.

Chalk

Calcium carbonate in the form of chalk, or whiting, does not need heating before grinding and is not caustic like calcium oxide. Although it is the remains of invertebrates from past ages, it has become a soft rock. It is easily broken up and ground with a pestle and mortar, using a small amount of water for lubrication.

Marble is chalk that has formed a harder rock. It may need to be processed in the same way as other hard rocks are (see p. 27); I have not used it. If it is heated, it is likely to change to calcium oxide and consequently be caustic to skin.

4 Glazes derived from rocks

Glazes will usually involve more than one material and are often combinations of rock dust and plant ash. In the examples in this chapter, materials from rock samples predominate.

Iron-rich glazes

Decomposed rocks or rock dusts high in iron can be ideal bases for rich, dark glazes like tenmoku, either on their own or combined with other materials. I am classifying as tenmoku any glaze that fires a deep, rich, brown colour. It can be fired in oxidation or reduction.

I have two bases for this glaze, which I use regularly. These two examples give an idea of what you can expect from iron-rich rocks. From my initial experiments, I found many results that I could have continued to explore, but chose the easiest to procure and process (see p. 55).

Example 1: Iron-rich rock-dust glaze

Lewisian gneiss is the main rock group found on the Outer Hebrides. Although it is banded and can look white, when fired it produces an iron-rich glaze. This rock is particular to the Outer Hebrides, but examples of iron-rich rocks are found globally. Fired alone to cone 8, this gneiss dust is matt to shiny brown, but combining it with a plant ash makes a rich, brown tenmoku glaze. Adding each of these five plant ashes makes five markedly different tenmokus: cereal straw, horsetail, nettle, driftwood and wrack seaweed.

The rock obviously has silica and alumina in it as it makes a fairly stable glaze at cone 8 to 10. Where the glaze is thick, a blue is associated with this dust, probably deriving from titanium. This gneiss dust can either be mixed with plant ashes or layered separately. See examples of this glaze on pp. 11 (vase), 36, 37, 39 (bowl detail), 44, 45, 46, 48, 49, 54, 55 (test 18), 63 and 103 (wee dram pots).

Example 2: Hornblende, degraded rock glaze

Degraded rocks of hornblende, in one state or another, form the subsoil where I live. Hornblende is a mineral described as one that comprises silica, alumina, calcium, mica and iron. This mica contains magnesium and, with calcium, is the source of flux in this glaze. The fired glaze has the characteristic 'buttery' surface texture associated with these fluxes.

When I was first directed to a deposit described as clay, I found it to be of little use as a clay body, though it could be regarded as a high-talc earthenware 'clay' with few plastic properties. It will make tiles and bricks, as seems to have been the case on the Isle of Lewis, where bricks renowned for their hardness were once manufactured. Such

Miranda Forrest, wee dram pot, 2007. Porcelain with slip-trailed decoration of peat ash. Iron ochre derived from peat ash is used to produce this celadon green (p. 59). Fired to cone 9 in reduction, 5.5 × 6.5 cm (2¼ × 2½ in.). *Photo: by the author.*

This pile of aggregate rock is Lewisian gneiss. It grinds to a grey-green dust that is used in Example 1 (p. 35). Growing through it are the spore-bearing 'flowers' of horsetail. This rock and this plant make the glaze on the wee dram pot shown! *Photo: by the author.*

Digging some degraded hornblende deposit found on a beach. *Photo: Graham Charlesworth.*

Miranda Forrest, three porcelain wee dram pots, 2010. From left: glaze from mixed wet measurements: 1 part gneiss dust, 1 part horsetail; mixed wet measurements of 2 parts gneiss dust, 1 part driftwood ash; and mixed wet measurements of 1 part gneiss dust, 1 part iron ochre, 1 part horsetail. All fired to cone 9 in reduction, 6 × 7 cm (2¼ × 2¾ in.). The same glazes on stoneware, in particular the wood ash example *(centre)*, will give a less bright and less runny result at the same temperature. *Photo: by the author.*

deposits, all over the Hebrides, were traditionally used to line the back of a fireplace. Local information such as this about native materials is always worth investigating and many clay-like deposits that are of little use as actual clay can be good as, or incorporated in, glazes.

At its best this hornblende makes a brown/black glaze that sparkles when the fine mica particles are caught by the light, and breaks to a lighter brown on edges when fired to cone 8 in oxidation. This glaze needs nothing added. It is a very amenable slip glaze to work with; on stoneware clay I have never seen it run, but on porcelain it occasionally does. Unfortunately, the many deposits of hornblende on the Outer Hebrides are not consistent as glazes and are variable even when dug from the same site. Some batches can produce an overly metallic, shiny brown glaze of little charm, which needs a reduction firing to at least cone 10 to become a glaze of any distinction. This is a reminder that it is worth testing any samples in oxidation, reduction and at different temperatures before discarding them. See an example of this glaze on p. 38.

Feldspar and granite glazes

Feldspar and granite rock dusts will need to be fired to see how they melt because they do not always conform to expectations. Some feldspars will turn quite dark when heated in a biscuit firing, yet then produce a glaze result with no iron, as shown in the photo at the top of p. 39. One that melts, or nearly melts, to a clear or opaque glaze at the temperature you most fire to opens up many possibilities. It can be used on its own; with an ochre as described on p. 38; it can be added to any glaze to help stabilise it; or it can be used with plant ashes for varying outcomes. See an example of this glaze on p. 69.

Sand as glaze

Sand can be such a variable material that it needs to be fired to see how it behaves. Unless it has seashell fragments in it, it is in effect a rock, and should be treated as such. To a large extent, my local sand is made up of silica grains, shell fragments and particles of iron-rich rock. It melts alone at about cone 6 to varying shades of brown. See examples of this glaze on pp. 40 (top left), 84, 91 and 100 (bottom).

Clay as glaze

Clay is arguably one of the easiest rock derivatives to process and use for a glaze. It will often melt on its own but, if it does not, a high-flux ash can be added. In general, found clays containing iron are more inclined to melt without an added flux, but there are no definite rules. If it fires red/brown at 1000°C (1832°F), rather than a pale colour, it has iron in it. A pale result may make it more flexible for experimenting with different plant ashes. Clay and ash combinations are probably the most common starting point for experiments. Examples of this glaze are shown on pp. 40 (top right), 41, 47 (bottom right), 65, 80, 81, 82, 83, 87, 89 (bottom), 97, 99 and 101.

Iron ochres

These natural iron ochres, in whatever form you have them, are a very versatile material and can be used in much the same way as purchased iron oxide. However, they are likely to be weaker, so tests need to be made to gauge the strength of colour. A small percentage in a glaze will give a honey colour when fired in oxidation and a green celadon when fired in reduction. A larger amount will make a tenmoku. Ochres give interesting finishes when brushed over or under plant ashes. See examples opposite (bottom right), and on pp. 14, 34, 37 (right), 59 (celadon), 61 (bottom), 64, 68, 76, 78 (left), 93, 94, 95, 102 and 109.

Miranda Forrest, stoneware serving platter, 2010. Hornblende glaze, dipped, with trailed horsetail ash decoration, fired to cone 10 in reduction, 6 × 27 cm (2½ × 10½ in.).
Photo: by the author.

Both these rock-dust test pieces gave a melted result when fired in reduction to cone 9. Both have horsetail ash layered on the left side. The test on the left contains a fragment of rock that looks dark; it looked like pink feldspar before it was heated for grinding. The horsetail ash seems incompatible on the left-hand piece, as it has not melted. The test on the right shows a result that originates from the 'yellow rock' (fourth from left) in the photograph on p. 18. *Photo: by the author.*

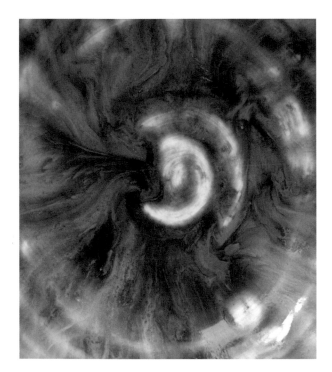

Miranda Forrest, porcelain bowl (detail), 2010. Brushed, layered glaze of gneiss dust, cereal straw ash, kelp ash. This detail shows a presumed titanium blue/green in the centre. Fired to cone 9 in reduction. *Photo: by the author.*

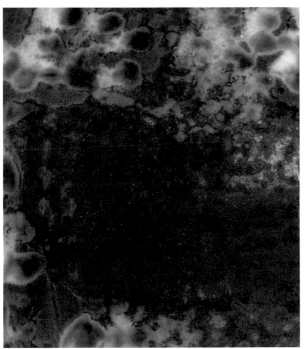

Miranda Forrest, bowl (detail), 2010. Stoneware. This detail shows the outside of a bowl, with iron ochre brushed on first and then yellow-flag-iris ash on top. *Photo: by the author.*

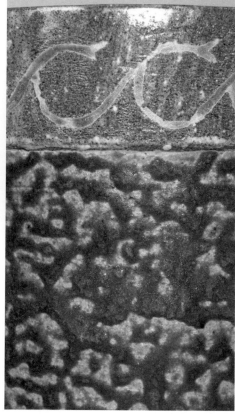

ABOVE LEFT: Louise Cook, stoneware tiles, 2012. Carved clay-stamp impressions are filled with different sands and fired to 1260°C (2300°F) in an electric kiln, each: 6.5 cm (2½ in.) square. *Photo: by the author.*

ABOVE: Barbara Attard Pettett, flowerpot (detail), 2008. Barbara, who lives on Malta, describes what this pot is made from: 'Buff stoneware clay painted with a slip made from sieved local Gozo clay and fired to 1260°C (2300°F). Incised Maltese design on the rim (inspired by carvings found in the Neolithic Temples in Tarxien, Malta) filled with Gozo clay slip and scraped back to reveal the design.' *Photo: Barbara Attard Pettett.*

LEFT: Fiona Byrne-Sutton, firing tests with Clackmannanshire glacial boulder clay, 2012. Left: unfired; centre: fired to 1160°C (2120°F); right: fired to 1260°C (2300°F), bog iron nodes now melting. *Photo: Amy Copeman.*

Miranda Forrest, bowl, 2010. Porcelain, fired to cone 8 in reduction. This bowl was glazed with a sample of the Gozo clay given to me by Barbara Attard Pettett. The glaze is layered, with clay brushed onto the biscuit-fired body as a slip, then a layer of South Uist nettle ash over the top, 10 × 21 cm (4 × 8 in.). *Photo: by the author.*

5 Glazes from plants and animals

Glazes from plant ashes

Plants have been grouped in this chapter by their dominant content. In the first section on land plants, examples are mainly herbaceous plants, with some examples using mixed wood ash. The second section covers marine plants.

Land plants

Silica-rich plant ashes

Rice-husk ash is the legendary silica-rich plant material used for the traditional chun glaze, which has an optical blue where it is applied thickly or pools. The blue is arguably caused by the scattering of light through the glaze. At one time it was thought to be reflecting off unmelted particles of silica suspended in the glaze, but is now thought to be from small amounts of phosphorus, a secondary glassmaker. Varying amounts of phosphorus are present in vegetation ashes and may be just as necessary as high levels of silica, or more so, to achieve the optical effect.

Grass family (*poaceae*, formerly *gramineae*) including cereals

As I do not live in Asia, where rice is grown in abundance, I looked for local plants in the same family to see if I could make a chun-type glaze. I found common reed, cereal straw and grass. All three have a wide global distribution.

LEFT: Miranda Forrest, vase, 2009. Stoneware, glaze layered by pouring: first layer cereal straw ash, second layer kelp ash. Fired to cone 9 in reduction, 13 × 11 cm (5 × 4½ in.).

RIGHT: In the Outer Hebrides, cereal crops are often cut and tied into sheaves in the traditional way. I have also used some of these crops preserved as silage and it seems to make no difference to the glaze result.
Photos: by the author.

When test-fired, reed and grass both remained a powder at cone 8, while cereal straw gave a dry glaze. This, indeed, suggested they are likely to be high in silica.

Reed and grass ash need a strong flux to melt them, such as that present in seaweed or wood ash, and must be mixed at the glaze-slops stage rather than layered or the result will be patchy. Results from reed produce the most blue – a pale blue where the glaze pools. Added feldspar will stabilise this glaze to give a pale blue/green over a larger area.

In the Outer Hebrides cereal crops are grown on the machair, a low-lying ground immediately inland of the coastal dunes, which is high in shell sand (calcium). I suspect the melting point of this cereal straw ash is affected because the cereal is grown on a calcium-rich soil, thereby increasing the calcium flux in it. It is possible that cereal straw in other areas may have a higher melting point and behave more like reed.

Examples of glazes containg reed ash can be seen on pp. 8, 10, 14, 47 (bottom left), 62, 66, 70, 71, 102 and 104. Glazes made from cereal straw are shown on pp. 10, 12, 39 (bottom left), 42, 44, 45, 46 (top), 49 (top), 51, 61 (top), 62, 63, 103, 105 and 110; an example of a glaze from grass is shown on p. 102.

Horsetail (*equisetaceae*) – found in America, Europe and Asia

I tested horsetail because it is an unusual plant with a reputedly high silica content. A member of the botanical division of flowerless plants, it is an ancient plant and has evolved little over a long period of time. It is found growing in wet, uncultivated or derelict areas of ground. It has an extensive root system that ranges far and deep.

The first test with horsetail ash alone produced a melted, creamy, greenish glaze with an optical blue in the centre, perhaps the most interesting single land-vegetation result to date. It also mixes well with other ashes and rock dusts. One of the other interesting effects associated with horsetail is carbon trapping during the firing, which gives a dark smoky colour to the glaze in places. Examples of horsetail glazes are included on pp. 10 (right), 11 (vase), 36 (top), 37, 38 (trailed decoration), 39 (top), 45, 46 (top), 47 (top, detail), 52, 57, 61 (top), 62, 68, 69 (bottom right), 73, 75, 103 (bottom), 105 and 110.

Miranda Forrest, stoneware handled servers, 2009. Left: cereal straw ash layered over gneiss dust makes a dark tenmoku that breaks lighter on edges. Right: poured cereal-straw-ash glaze only; cereal-straw ash makes a dry glaze when applied on its own. Fired to cone 8 in oxidation, 10 × 20 cm (4 × 8 in.). *Photo: by the author.*

These two pieces are interesting because only three glaze materials are used between them.

RIGHT: Front: Miranda Forrest, bowl, 2011. Stoneware, poured glaze from mixed wet measurements of 1 part gneiss dust, 1 part horsetail. Fired to cone 9 in reduction, 7 × 15 cm (3 × 6 in.).
Behind: Miranda Forrest, platter, 2010. Porcelain, glaze layered by pouring: first layer gneiss dust, second layer cereal straw ash, third layer horsetail ash. Layering this glaze gives a hazy depth to the fired piece, quite different to the results of applying the same ingredients as mixed glaze slops (see the yellow bowl, top of p. 46). A presumed 'titanium' blue associated with the rock dust is in the centre. Fired to cone 10 in reduction, 4 × 33 cm (1½ × 13 in.). *Photo: by the author.*

Plant ashes with flux

Many plants contain small amounts of elements like phosphorus and iron in sufficient quantities to influence a glaze. High-flux plant ashes give a stringy effect, the result of the glaze flowing down the clay surface as it melts. It indicates an unbalanced glaze, too high in flux, though it does produce an interesting surface texture. If a glaze is too runny, add some alumina to stabilise it. Wood ash is the traditional material associated with this glaze but I have found plants from the iris (yellow flag iris) and polygonaceae (Japanese knotweed) familes also produce this effect (see also marine vegetation ash, pp. 48–50).

Many plant ashes contain flux, and also iron, in sufficient quantity to influence a glaze. I find nettle ash is particularly notable for a green result from iron.

Examples of different kinds of high-flux plant ash glazes are shown on the following pages: dock, p. 62; iris, pp. 14, 39 (bottom right), 47 (bottom), 62, 102, 103 (bottom), and 110; Japanese knotweed, pp. 47 (bottom right) and 75; nettle, pp. 41, 48, 50, 68 and 105; thistle, pp. 47 (top right), 52 and 62 (top); wild angelica, pp. 62 (top) and 106; wood ash, driftwood, pp. 8, 37 (centre), 62 (top), 66, 70, 71 and 104; wood ash, pp. 87, 89, 96 and 98.

LEFT, TOP: Miranda Forrest, porcelain bowl, 2011. This yellow glaze has the same ingredients as the platter on p. 45, but is mixed, not layered. Poured glaze from mixed wet measurements of 1 part gneiss dust, 1 part cereal-straw ash, 1 part horsetail ash. Fired to cone 9 in reduction, 8 × 13 cm (3 × 5½ in.).

LEFT, BOTTOM: Miranda Forrest, bowl, 2009. Stoneware, layered glaze poured on: first layer gneiss dust, second layer yellow-flag-iris ash. Fired to cone 8 in reduction, 7 × 19 cm (2¾ × 9½ in.).

RIGHT, TOP: Miranda Forrest, bowl (detail), 2010. Porcelain, layered glaze brushed on: first layer thistle ash, second layer horsetail. Fired to cone 8 in reduction.

BELOW: Miranda Forrest, tea bowl, 2010. Stoneware, with reed and kelp glaze showing pale blue where thick. The proportions of this glaze were not precisely recorded and it was superseded by wood ash and reed as a less problematical glaze (see p. 62, two goblets shown on right). Fired to cone 10 in reduction, 8 × 9 cm (3 × 3½ in.).

RIGHT: Miranda Forrest, vase, 2011. Stoneware, with glaze from mixed wet measurements of 1 part Sussex native clay, 1 part Japanese knotweed ash, brushed on. Fired to cone 8 in reduction, 6 × 6.5 cm (2½ ×2¾ in.). *Photos: by the author.*

Marine vegetation ash high in flux

Kelp

Historically, seaweeds have been collected for use in the glass and ceramics industry. Tangle, or oarweed, is the variety I have used in all experiments with kelp seaweed.

It is apparent that kelp ashes contain a lot of water-soluble salts, so much so that the water absorbed into the clay walls can affect the glaze on the other side and, in extreme cases, make the whole structure 'bubble up' and deform.

When the slops are applied by pouring *into* a biscuit-fired bowl and then again *onto* the outside, it seems that where there is a build-up of salts carried in with the water from both sides, this can cause a whole section to explode off during the firing ascent between 400 and 600°C (752 and 1112°F). This appears to happen on thinly thrown bowls made using a fine clay (see opposite). I have not seen more robust stoneware clay bodies, so far, suffer this problem (see p. 51).

As this ash is high in water-soluble salts, there is a case for 'washing' the ash. After various experiments, I now use kelp ash unwashed, applied sparingly and only on one side of thin clay walls. It should be noted that there could be issues with these salts contaminating the insides of kilns if a lot of seaweed is used. Using a relatively small amount of seaweed, I have not so far had a problem.

Kelp-ash glazes will run freely and produce interesting blue/green/yellow hues with crackle effects where it pools. Examples can be seen on pp. 10 (top left), 12, 42, 47 (bottom left), 49 (both) and 51.

Miranda Forrest, bowl, 2010. Porcelain, with layered glaze: first layer nettle ash, second layer gneiss dust. Fired to cone 9 in reduction, 10 × 21 cm (4 × 8 in.). *Photo: by the author.*

RIGHT: Miranda Forrest, bowl, 2008. Stoneware with layered glaze: first layer gneiss dust, second cereal straw ash, third kelp ash. Fired to cone 9 in reduction, 7 × 20 cm (2¾ × 8 in.). This is one of the few survivors of my first firing of larger bowls with kelp ash. It survived because it only had kelp ash applied on one side. A cratered effect from the kelp ash can be seen on some parts of it.

BELOW: Miranda Forrest, bowl, 2009. Fine white throwing stoneware, 'exploded' by soluble salts in kelp-ash water. Fired to cone 10 in reduction, 10 × 25 cm (4 × 10 in.). *Photos: by the author.*

Wracks and other seaweeds

The majority of wracks will make a glaze, but my results from different species are so similar that it has become not worth separating them: all form a pale cream glaze in oxidation and a greener one in reduction.

They are strong sources of potassium and sodium flux. For instance, a ratio of just one wet measurement of wrack to nine of gneiss dust is all that is needed for a glaze. Like kelp, wrack seaweeds contain water-soluble salts, so the same warnings apply; however, wrack does seem less troublesome to use. Examples can be seen right, and on pp. 14, 102 and 105.

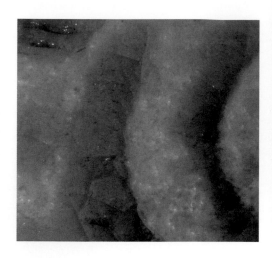

Glazes derived from animals

Seashells are the only source of flux I can collect locally that does not contain any iron (all my plant ash results show some iron in them). Mixed with equal quantities of feldspar, seashells make a white, crazed glaze on porcelain.

Chalk or whiting is not local to me, but samples layered over gneiss dust give a similar effect to those using some plant ashes. Chalk can also be a source of flux without iron. An example of a glaze made from shells is below; chalk/whiting glazes can be seen on pp. 99 (bottom right) and 101.

Miranda Forrest, bowl (detail), 2010. Porcelain, with poured glaze from mixed wet measurements of 9 parts nettle, 1 part seaweed. It has a sparkly strong green where it pools. Fired to cone 8 in reduction.

LEFT: Miranda Forrest, vase, 2011. Porcelain, with glaze from mixed wet measurements of 1 part potash feldspar (purchased), 1 part ground seashells, 1 part nettle ash. Fired to cone 9 in reduction, 4.5 × 7 cm (1¾ × 2¾ in.).

RIGHT: Miranda Forrest, landscape sculpture, 2009. This piece was thrown using grogged white stoneware clay. Poured glaze in layers: first layer cereal straw ash, second layer kelp ash. Fired to cone 10 in reduction, 90 × 24 cm (35½ × 9½ in.). *Photos: by the author.*

<table>
<tr><td>

6

</td><td>

Making your glaze

</td></tr>
</table>

Testing methods

These are guidelines by which you can develop your own glazes. If you wish to start with wide-ranging experiments to see what glaze materials are available in your locality, then start with batches of tests, as I did. Alternatively, I have suggested a 'five materials test' for those who would prefer to start with fewer materials. Obviously these tests can be adapted to suit your own working methods. There is also a section on experiments at earthenware temperatures.

Batch tests of many single materials

I test the majority of samples as a single material fired to cone 8 to 10 (approximately 1260–1300°C (2300–2372°F), my normal production temperature range. I make test saucers about 5 cm (2 in.) in diameter, with rims to stop any glaze spilling onto kiln shelves (see pp. 54–5). See also p. 64 for stamped test pieces.

After firing, I label all test pieces, which enables samples that are initially discarded to be revisited when a better understanding of the body of work opens up other

LEFT: Miranda Forrest, pedestal bowl, 2011. Porcelain, with glaze from mixed wet measurements of 1 part 'cone 8' base glaze, 1 part horsetail ash, 1 part thistle ash. Fired to cone 9 in reduction, 9.5 × 15 cm (3¾ × 6 in.).

RIGHT: A selection of 10 cm (4 in.) test bowls. See p. 56, second-phase tests.
Photos: by the author.

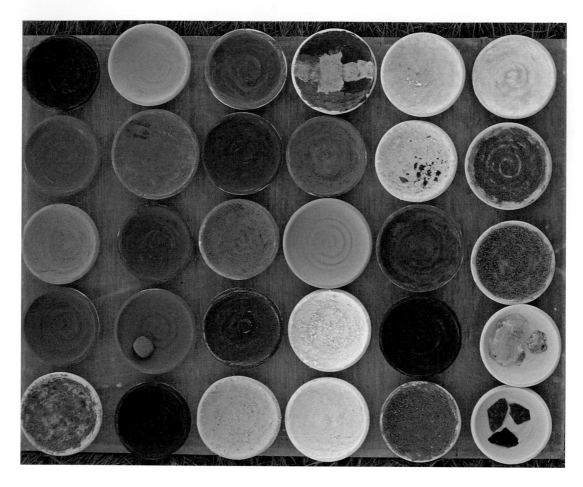

A batch of unfired tests.
Photo: by the author.

possibilities. It is important to log all information as memory is fallible. I tend to work in batches and number all pieces by scratching into damp clay at the green (unfired) stage. These numbers are then used as a reference to log the glaze details in a notebook at the time it is applied. After firing, the information is transferred to the unglazed base using a permanent marker. Alternatively, paint this information onto the base using an iron oxide at the time of glazing. Work out a method that suits you and use it diligently.

When you do a batch of different test samples like the ones illustrated here, the results will give you information as to whether the sample remains unchanged, melts or completely disappears, while the colour will indicate what oxides may be present. For those samples that melt, the extent and type of melt is also informative. A further consideration before continuing experiments with a particular sample is how easy or time-consuming it is to process.

I fire a range of materials because that is the only way to find out what the result will be. I get a lot of iron-rich test results and from these I choose to continue only with those results I like and that are also easy to process. For this latter reason, I have not continued to develop many of the tests in the batch illustrated (above and opposite).

The results after firing the tests opposite to cone 8 in oxidation. Starting top left and reading vertically: 1 ditch ochre, 2 reed ash, 3 cereal straw ash, 4 red olivine, 5 beach deposit, 6 iris ash, 7 nettle ash, 8 reed ash, 9 possible clay, 10 iron ochre, 11 green olivine, 12 roadside deposit, 13 Welsh slate, 14 Welsh cereal straw, 15 Welsh sand, 16 layered combinations of 13, 14 and 15, 17 roadside olivine, 18 gneiss dust (fine), 19 sheet rock, 20 white, soft rock, 21 feldspar (A), 22 feldspar (B), 23 bog deposit, 24 road-cutting iron, 25 road-cutting deposit, 26 white stone, 27 outcrop fragments, 28 gneiss dust (coarse), 29 white mica, 30 black mica. *Photo: by the author.*

The two photos show a batch of test samples, unfired and fired (cone 8 in oxidation). This is one of the first batches of tests I did to discover what was available in my locality. The tests are numbered, starting with 1 in the top left-hand corner and ending with 30 in the bottom right-hand corner. If you do a wide-ranging batch-test, fired to these temperatures (cone 8 to 10), similar results are likely. From these results, the following are suggestions for the next stage of experiments.

Rock sources
Test any of the rock sources, including clay, described in Chapter 2. These are all likely to have silica and alumina in them but varying amounts of flux. If a rock-derived

sample shows signs of melting, then for the next experiment I try it with a plant ash. Layer or mix it with different plant ashes that also show signs of melting, or whiting (calcium) from chalk or shells. Samples like clay may be quite dry, while kaolin will be a dull white, but they are still worth further experiments.

All my easy-to-process rock samples are iron-rich. I continued with no.18, the gneiss dust described in Chapter 4 (p. 35, example 1). Nos. 21 and 22 have melted; these two are feldspar from defunct feldspar quarries. These feldspar samples were rendered to small fragments with a hammer for testing. I find feldspar is too hard to grind without prior heating (see p. 27).

Plant sources

Generally, plant ashes that remain as a powder after firing are high in silica and will need a strong flux to melt them. They also need to be mixed rather than layered. Mix them with the strongest flux you have. I find wood ash is the best but kelp ash also works. Test nos. 2 and 8 are both reed ashes.

Plant ashes that melt are the ones to try with rock samples, as suggested above. Also try them with other ashes, iron ochres and whiting.

The following samples are referred to in many of the glazes illustrated in this book. No. 3, cereal straw ash, is partly melted, giving a dry-textured matt glaze. No. 6 is iris (yellow flag) and no. 7 is nettle. These are both shiny and show some green.

Animal sources

Tests from high-calcium animal sources are unlikely to melt. Chalk forms a thin brittle sheet when fired alone but when incorporated with rock or plant materials it behaves as flux. Seashells are the only flux I have that fires white, as my fluxing plant ashes all seem to have some iron in them. Shells fired to 1000°C (1832°F) are shown on p. 28, top right; fired to 1260°C (2300°F) they change little.

Second-phase tests

If you try these ideas for tests by layering or mixing them on more test saucers, an understanding of what works will begin to emerge. With a two-ash test, you can put an iron-bearing sample over a third of it to give you more information.

After doing this, any results that I find interesting I try on small bowls about 10 cm (4 in.) in diameter. Glazes are only put on the inside so as to protect kiln shelves from runs. A glaze will behave differently on vertical and horizontal surfaces and depending on whether it is applied thinly or thickly. This is partly illustrated in the photograph of my 10 cm (4 in.) test bowls where the glaze has pooled in the centre (p. 53). My second-phase test saucers and small bowls are all stoneware and fired to cone 8 to 10 in reduction or oxidation.

Five materials test: stoneware

An alternative method of testing is to combine the first- and second-phase tests but using only a few samples, say five, overlaying them to try and find a result in a single test firing. This test is designed to be fired to stoneware temperatures, preferably but not necessarily in reduction, as this will be dependent on the type of kiln you have.

These photographs illustrate a set of tests carried out to explore different rocks in my neighbourhood. Unheated rocks are shown on the left, in the same layout as the fired (cone 9, in reduction) test results shown on the right. Each saucer had some of the individual heated and ground rock poured on as glaze slops, then a layer of horsetail ash over only the left-hand side of each test. *Photo: by the author.*

Choose two degraded rock samples.

First choose one iron-rich material – iron ochre, subsoil, iron-rich rock dust or clay. Process the sample by passing it, if possible, through a 60-mesh sieve, and by mixing it with water until the solution reaches the consistency of single cream. If the rock sample is granular rather than dust, it may be easier to spoon it onto the test saucer instead of brushing it.

Then take one iron-free material – try either a rock sample or sand that you think will fire white. Process the rock sample in the same way as the iron-rich one.

Choose three ash samples

It is a good idea to try ashes of plants from different families, such as wood ash, nettle ash, Japanese knotweed/dock ash, cereal straw/reed ash, and thistle/borage ash; refer to the table on p. 23. You might try any plant that is locally abundant, easy to collect, or just of personal interest. You will need to collect approximately 1kg (2lb) of each herbaceous material, render it into ashes and sieve it per instructions. You are aiming for single cream consistency, so be careful not to add too much water (see p. 30).

Five sample glaze test table

15 iron sample iron-free sample ←				
13 iron sample corn ash	**14** iron-free sample corn ash ←			
10 iron sample nettle ash	**11** iron-free sample nettle ash	**12** corn ash nettle ash ←		
6 iron sample wood ash	**7** iron-free sample wood ash	**8** corn ash wood ash	**9** nettle ash wood ash ←	
1 iron sample	**2** iron-free sample	**3** corn ash	**4** nettle ash	**5** wood ash

NB: If you use reed ash it is better to mix it, not layer it. If you do layer it, it will still give some results but must go on as the base layer. Mix equal quantities, e.g. one teaspoon, or one part, of each material.

The test requires 15 test saucers (biscuit-fired) with a rim to prevent the glaze running onto the kiln shelves. Saucers about 5 cm (2 in.) in diameter will give you enough information without requiring too much glaze. They should be numbered before biscuit firing.

Lay out the test saucers following the numbers in the grid above. The first row has only one sample tested on each saucer (numbers 1 to 5). Rows 2 to 5 all have two samples on each saucer.

Starting on the left with test 1, brush on the iron-bearing sample chosen. Continue with the iron sample up the column, so this is brushed onto numbers 1, 6, 10, 13 and 15. Wash and dry the brush thoroughly, especially if you are only using one brush. Move onto the next column – in this example, the iron-free rock or sand sample. Follow the arrows so that it is put onto numbers 2, 7, 11, 14 and 15. Continue with the test, ensuring you wash and dry the brush between samples, or when it has brushed over the top of another sample, to prevent cross-contamination. You will get extra information if each sample is put on more thickly in one area of the saucer.

Use the numbers on the base of each saucer to keep a record of all tests in a notebook. Include information such as any problems brushing on a sample, whether it has gone on too thickly or thinly, and whether it is easy to use. This may be very useful for later reference.

When the test saucers come out of the kiln, write on the back with a permanent marker information such as what was put onto them, the firing temperature, and whether it was in reduction or oxidation. Obviously some sort of shorthand has to be used; decide on a system and use it consistently. A batch or firing number is also helpful.

When you have found some results that interest you, try them on larger pieces. Remember that they may run so protect the kiln shelves; soft firebrick is very good for collecting drips (see p. 70).

The most stable glazes produced will be the ones that have a balance of the three glaze ingredients: silica, alumina and flux. These are likely to be the ones that have some rock materials in them, because of their alumina content.

Layering remains my preference for some of my glazes – generally, an ochre over ash, or an ash over an iron-rich rock dust or clay. The latter gives the typical, stringy ash glaze that, if stabilised too much, would defeat the object. The knack is to get it to run but not so much that it falls off the pot!

Combining collected material with purchased materials

My driftwood and reed glaze, made of ashes alone, gives a white glaze with an optical blue that I cherish, but it is inclined to run because of a lack of alumina, the stabiliser. If glazes run and pool too much, adding some feldspar should reduce this. I have rocks that will fire white, but they do require involved processing, so sometimes it is easier to use a purchased source of alumina.

In the end it comes down to personal taste and circumstances – how much of the glaze you want to be made from what you have collected and how well you feel the glaze works – as to whether you want to stay with collected materials alone or add some purchased ones. You may feel adding just one collected material to a purchased base glaze is enough to personalise it.

This is also the stage when the decision is taken about how to measure quantities of materials – whether you want to do more exact tests with dry materials or are happy with wet measuring. My work continues with wet measurements.

Adding to a base glaze

If you have your own base glaze, try some experiments with that. Alternatively, try Bernard Leach's 'cone 8' base glaze. The recipe (by dry weight) is potash feldspar 40%, flint/quartz 30%, whiting 20%, kaolin/china clay 10%. This recipe is taken from *A Potter's Book* by Bernard Leach. I mix up a batch of it to the consistency of single cream and then use spoons/ladles to measure. This glaze has a maturing range of cone 8 to 10. It is inclined to craze.

Celadon

A celadon glaze has a small percentage of iron (less than 2%) in it, which makes a pale green glaze when fired in reduction and a honey colour in oxidation. Try any source of iron in a base glaze. I make a celadon by adding peat ash to the 'cone 8' base glaze described above. I decide how much to put in by the colour of the raw glaze, but it is roughly seven wet measures, or parts, of 'cone 8' to three of peat ash (the iron in peat ash is not very strong). See the photo on p. 60.

LEFT: Here, a sample of wet peat ash is shown on the left, and on the right, peat ash added to Bernard Leach's 'cone 8' base glaze, at the strength I use for a celadon. In the middle, the sample is not quite strong enough and needs a little more peat ash added. This qualitative colour guide works for me, but dry-weighing and testing would work, too.

A line-blend test is a useful experiment for discovering how two materials, e.g. a base glaze and iron ochre, change depending on their ratios, but try any of your natural glazes/materials with a base glaze. If you do not want to do a line blend, experiment with wet measurements in the ratio of 1 or 2 parts ash to 1 part base glaze.

RIGHT: Miranda Forrest, footed bowl, 2010. Porcelain, with glaze from mixed wet measurements of 1 part 'cone 8' base glaze, 1 part horsetail ash, 1 part cereal straw ash. The dark colour is the result of carbon trapping, associated with the horsetail ash. Fired to cone 9 in reduction, 8.5 × 17 cm (3½ × 6¾ in.).
Photos: by the author.

Line blend test

Base glaze	90	80	70	60	50	40	30	20	10
Iron ochre	+ 10	+ 20	+ 30	+ 40	+ 50	+ 60	+ 70	+ 80	+ 90
Total in test glaze	= 100 1	= 100 2	= 100 3	= 100 4	= 100 5	= 100 6	= 100 7	= 100 8	= 100 9

The measurements in the table above are given in percentages; measurements can be made by weight if dry, or by volume if wet.

Adding a feldspar

If you're using a purchased feldspar there are several to choose from. Remember that Cornish stone and nepheline syenite come into the feldspar family. Cornish stone is high in silica, whereas nepheline syenite has the highest alumina of the feldspars. Potash feldspar, soda feldspar and lime (calcium) feldspar are the other usual choices.

Purchased clay bodies used for tests

High-firing clays, including different porcelains, are suitable for experiments, and this is what I have used for the majority of tests at stoneware temperatures. I find that porcelain will sometimes distort at my top temperatures (1300°C/2372°F), particularly in association with kelp ash (p. 12), and glazes on porcelain are more inclined to run. I use a heavily grogged stoneware clay, of the kind usually employed for handbuilding, for large forms. This clay tends to absorb glaze during firing and so produces glazes with a more matt finish; it can be termed 'thirsty' (examples are shown on pp. 6, 51 and 63). A white stoneware is used for the smaller thrown pieces.

RIGHT: Miranda Forrest, two wee dram pots, 2007. Both are examples of the celadon glaze described on p. 59, applied by dipping. The pot on the left is porcelain with a slip-trailed decoration of pure peat ash that has melted into the glaze underneath. The pot on the right is stoneware; the difference the clay makes is obvious. Both were fired to cone 9 in reduction, left: 5.5 × 6.5 cm (2¼ × 2½ in.), right: 6.5 × 7.5 cm (2½ × 3 cm). *Photo: by the author.*

ABOVE: Miranda Forrest, various pieces, 2011. From left to right: (1) wee dram pot, porcelain, with glaze from mixed wet measurements of 2 parts potash feldspar (purchased), 1 part horsetail ash, 1 part iris ash (yellow flag), 1 part cereal straw ash; (2) blue tea bowl, porcellaneous stoneware, with glaze from mixed wet measurements of 1 part 'cone 8' glaze base, 1 part horsetail ash, 1 part thistle ash; (3) vase, porcelain, with glaze from mixed wet measurements of 1 part 'cone 8' base glaze, 1 part wild angelica ash; (4) vase, porcelain, with glaze from mixed wet measurements of 1 part 'cone 8' base glaze, 1 part dock ash; (5) goblet, porcelain and (6) goblet, porcellanous stoneware, both with poured glaze from mixed wet measurements of 1 part potash feldspar (purchased), 1 part driftwood ash, 1 part reed ash. This reed-ash glaze can have quite deep-blue flashes where thicker. All six pieces fired to cone 9/10 in reduction, from 6–10 cm (2½–4 in.) high × 7–10 cm (2¾–4 in.) wide. *Photo: by the author.*

LEFT: Miranda Forrest, small vase (left) and tea bowl (right), 2011. Small vase: porcelain, with poured glaze from mixed wet measurements of 1 part Cornish stone (purchased), 1 part horsetail ash, 1 part yellow flag iris ash, 1 part cereal straw ash. Fired to cone 8 in reduction, 4.5 × 6.5 cm (1¾ × 2½ in.). Tea bowl: porcellanous stoneware, with poured glaze from mixed wet measurements of 1 part potash feldspar (purchased), 1 part horsetail ash, 1 part yellow flag iris ash, 1 part cereal straw ash. Fired to cone 9+ in reduction, 7 × 8 cm (2¾ × 3¼ in.).

ABOVE: Miranda Forrest, landscape sculpture, 2009. Thrown from white grogged stoneware clay, this clay has affected the glaze of gneiss dust and cereal straw ash to give it a matt result. Compare it with the glaze on the handled server on p. 44. The glaze was poured onto the pot to achieve an irregular finish, fired to cone 10 in reduction, 89 × 23 cm (35 × 9 in.). *Photos: by the author.*

These earthenware samples are stamped, but still have the edges turned up to stop glaze getting onto kiln shelves. All fired to 1050°C (2012°F) in a gas kiln either in reduction or oxidation using the glazes described below, on this page.
Photo: by the author.

Earthenware

For earthenware tests in this book, I have used a white earthenware clay body.

A drawback regarding natural glazes at earthenware temperatures is that, unfortunately, the fluxes capable of melting silica at low temperatures are highly toxic in the raw state. In ceramics, we therefore use lead and borax as a frit. I cannot advise you to do other than use these frits as a base to which collected materials may be added, though lead is not now used in any form in some parts of the world. When glaze materials that are unsafe to use raw are melted and re-solidified, they become safer to use, a process known as fritting. Fritting is usually carried out industrially.

I have done some tests to temperatures between 1050 and 1170°C (2012 and 1238°F). The clear glazes for these tests are:

1. Lead frit 85%, kaolin (china clay) 15% by dry weight.

2. Alkaline frit 85%, kaolin (china clay) 15% by dry weight. Temperatures higher than 1100°C (2012°F) will overfire this glaze and give a crackle effect.

BELOW: Miranda Forrest, pots, 2011. Left and right: earthenware, with brushed glaze from mixed wet measurements of 1 part alkaline frit glaze, 1 part found iron ochre; left pot reduction-fired, right pot oxidation-fired, both to 1050°C (2012°F), diameter: 10 cm (4 in.). Centre: earthenware, with brushed, layered glazed: first layer found iron ochre, second layer alkaline frit glaze. Fired in an electric kiln to 1100°C (2012°F), diameter: 10 cm (4 in.).
Photo: by the author.

Miranda Forrest, vases, 2011. These three earthenware pieces were brushed with a slip made from the clay deposit described in Chapter 8 (p. 74, 75) and biscuit-fired to 1180°C (2156°F). Rear: alkaline glaze (inside only); front left: alkaline glaze; front right: lead glaze. All fired to 1050°C (2012°F), front pieces 15 cm (6 in.) high. *Photo: by the author.*

I have experimented with iron-based materials and some ashes. I find that the plants that work best are the ones that have the finest ashes after burning. Both iris ash and Japanese knotweed ash melt in with the two glazes at 1170°C (1238°F), but not at the lower temperatures. Mixing ashes works better than layering them but they need to be mixed well. I find that plant ashes with high silica and, surprisingly, marine ashes do not melt at this temperature.

Iron ochre and peat ash work, while rock samples do not. Found clay slip can also be brushed on raw clay and burnished, or glazed over the top. Iron will give colours ranging from a natural brown to a yellow in oxidation and a green in reduction.

Miscellaneous materials

Glass

Any found glass can be fired. It will melt and re-solidify, with crazing, at earthenware and stoneware temperatures. Coloured glass usually retains its colour although reds can burn out at high temperatures. Glass slumps at about 850°C (1562°F) and will flow at higher temperatures.

Miranda Forrest, goblet, 2011. Porcellaneous stoneware, poured glaze from mixed wet measurements of 1 part potash feldspar (purchased), 1 part driftwood ash, 1 part reed ash. This reed-driftwood-ash glaze varies in the intensity of blue or green colour depending on clay body, thickness of glaze and firing temperature. Fired to cone 10 in reduction, 7.5 × 7.5 cm (3 × 3 in.). *Photo: by the author.*

7

Glaze application and firing

I store glaze materials individually, only mixing or layering them with other materials as required. I find this a more flexible way of working than mixing glaze slops in bulk. This also seems to eliminate problems, such as deflocculating, which can occur if glaze slops are stored, mixed, for any length of time. 'Deflocculating' is a term that describes the individual particles, suspended in the glaze slops, being held apart from each other. This makes the glaze slops look thicker than they are, and consequently too much water can be added by mistake. If the glaze slops are too thin, too few particles will be deposited on the biscuited ware when the glaze slops are applied. Washing ashes (before mixing them into a glaze slop) can help prevent deflocculating (see p. 32).

Glaze slops

Incorporating either purchased ground feldspar or a base glaze with natural materials will help keep glaze slops suspended and make them easier to apply. As a general principle, the finer the particles in glaze slops, the better they will remain suspended. To remix the slops if they have settled out, pour off the water and retain it. Slice the sediment with a flat, looped turning tool, return the water, and you will find it easier to mix up with a balloon whisk.

Collection of utensils used in the process of glaze slops application. The loop turning tool balanced on the containers is excellent for slicing settled glaze particles. These measuring spoons are ideal for measuring small amounts of wet glaze slops materials. Jugs can be used for larger amounts. *Photo: by the author.*

Miranda Forrest, tea bowls, 2011. Both stoneware, with brushed glazed from mixed measurements of 1 part 'cone 8' base glaze, 1 part horsetail ash, 1 part nettle ash. The tea bowl on the left has iron ochre brushed on under the glaze, while the one on the right has it brushed on top. Iron ochre can provide greater visual interest in the fired glaze when brushed on unevenly. Fired to cone 9 in reduction, 8 × 9 cm (3¼ × 3½ in.). *Photo: by the author.*

Glaze application

These natural glaze materials are not as easy as conventional glaze materials to get onto the biscuit-fired surface, particularly if they have not been finely ground or ball-milled.

Brushing

I find brushing on the glaze materials is the best method for small pieces or when touching up. It allows more control of water into the biscuited body. Quantities of glaze slops that are too small for dipping can still be brushed on.

Dipping and pouring

I usually combine these two methods. Have sufficient glaze slops in a container large enough to immerse the piece you are intending to glaze. Pick up the piece in one hand by the base, collect some glaze slops in a jug and pour them into the piece to apply the glaze on the inside. Then pour the glaze slops from the piece back into the container. The piece, now upside down, should be immediately but carefully dipped into the glaze slops. This leaves the base unglazed. This method can only be used if there are enough glaze slops to dip the piece, but it does give the most even coverage. If there are insufficient glaze slops for dipping the outside of the piece, the glaze can be poured on. This may result in double thicknesses but these can be gently scraped down while still damp if desired. Touch up any areas not sufficiently covered with a brush. Particles in the glaze slops should be kept suspended by stirring them regularly with a balloon whisk.

A drawback to dipping or pouring glaze slops containing marine vegetation ash is that water containing too many soluble salts can be absorbed into the biscuited body (see pp. 48 and 49).

As a guide, you are aiming for a thickness of applied glaze on the biscuited body of anything up to, but no more than, about 3 mm. Experience and personal preference will inform the choices you make as to the thickness and application method. Some degraded rock and slip glazes are very amenable and a joy to work with, while kelp ash in particular can never be described as such!

LEFT: A large vessel with glaze slops newly applied by pouring. To facilitate this method on a large piece, start by putting a bucket on the floor. Place two flat wooden batons across the top to support a small 'turntable' or 'whirler', and place the piece to be glazed on top of this. The whirler allows the piece to be rotated while glaze slops are poured onto it. The bucket collects excess slops. This vessel has nettle ash as a base layer and horsetail ash on top. The top layer is yet to be scraped down where it is too thick, prior to touching up with a brush. Note the indent or gully at the base of the 'neck'. This is intended for glaze to collect in during firing. Horsetail ash gives a blue where thick, but it runs on vertical surfaces, so it is only in the gully that any blue is anticipated. This vessel is thrown with a high-grog stoneware clay. Height: 67 cm (27 in.). *Photo by the author.*

ABOVE: This glaze ran but was caught by the piece of soft firebrick. *Photo: by the author.*

ABOVE: Miranda Forrest, small dish, 2012. Stoneware, with glaze from mixed wet measurements of 1 part 'yellow rock', 1 part horsetail, applied thickly. See p. 39, top right. Fired to cone 9 in reduction, 1.5 × 7.5 cm (¾ × 3 in.). *Photos: by the author*

Miranda Forrest, curly tail platter, 2011. Stoneware, with glaze from mixed wet measurements of 1 part potash feldspar (purchased), 1 part driftwood ash, 1 part reed ash. Fired to cone 9 in reduction, 6 × 20 cm (2½ × 8 in.). *Photo: by the author.*

Packing the kiln

Natural glazes' propensity to run during firing means that some thought has to be put into how to stop them sticking to the kiln shelves. When glazes are first tested on vertical surfaces, always put them on the inside of a vessel or put the test piece with glaze on it in a sacrificial biscuit fired saucer. At the experimental stage, and until I am sure that a glaze does not run, I fire all pieces that are glazed on the outside on soft firebrick. These can be cut to size with a hand saw (do not inhale the dust). This soft firebrick absorbs glaze very well and allows drips to be ground off after firing (see photo top right p. 69). I have not found using old/second-hand kiln shelves with a deep bed of alumina or silica sand to be as satisfactory as soft fire brick. Silicon carbide kiln shelves are available in some countries, and are reputed to be very good for not sticking, but I have not used them.

Firing the kiln

A firing that does not restrict oxygen throughout the firing cycle is called an 'oxidation' firing. The restriction of oxygen in the kiln atmosphere during part of the firing is called a reduction firing. For a reduction firing, a fuel producing a flame is traditionally used to heat the kiln.

I use Standard (large) Orton cones for determining the temperature, backed up by a pyrometer. All my high-temperature firings were carried out in a gas-fired kiln. All high-fired ceramics were biscuit-fired to 1000°C (1832°F).

I aim to take glaze firings up at a steady 200°C (360°F) per hour, though it is possible to increase the speed of the temperature rise if there are no marine vegetation ash glazes in the kiln (see pp. 48 and 49, bottom). A soak of 15 minutes at top temperature is optional and depends on the length of firing and how densely you have packed the kiln. I find a densely packed kiln has a slower temperature rise, which reduces the need for a soak. For a reduction firing, reduction is started at 950°C (1742°F) and stopped about 40°C (72°F) below top temperature, whereupon the firing is completed in oxidation. Once the kiln has been turned off, all bungs are closed and it is left to cool, which takes about 14 hours. Only when the temperature is below 200°C (392°F) do I open

Miranda Forrest, bowl, 2011. Porcelain, with glaze from mixed wet measurements of 1 part potash feldspar (purchased), 1 part driftwood ash, 1 part reed ash. Fired to cone 9 in reduction, 8 × 13 cm (3 × 5½ in.). *Photo: by the author.*

the kiln door a 'crack', just enough to look inside. I allow the ware another hour or so to cool before unpacking it.

My kiln is rather uneven in temperature: when cone 8 has gone down at the top spy-hole, cone 10 will be just starting to bend in a hotter part, and at the bottom cone 8 will only just be going. Cones in different parts of your kiln will tell you how evenly it is firing.

Problem solving

The main problem I have found with natural glazes is running during firing. Some of this is addressed by the solution, given previously, of adding a stabiliser, but until a glaze has been fired many times and not run, I fire it on soft firebrick (see p. 69). Sometimes the effect of the glaze running is a desirable one, as the pooling can give lovely effects, as shown above. Some thought can also be put into the design of the piece to give the glaze a place to pool. An incised line at the foot, or a small ledge, is enough to catch the glaze and prevent it overflowing. This can be seen in some of the forms illustrated, where the glaze has pooled to a greater or lesser extent. Examples of incised lines can be seen on pp. 8, 46, 52, 66, 71 and 102; examples of ledges on pp. 7, 11, 14, 36 (top), 37, 41, 45 (bowl), 47 (bottom), 50 (bottom), 62, 68, 106 and 110.

Lowering the temperature can lessen a glaze's tendency to run, but this can also affect the result in other ways. Conversely, if a glaze is not melting, try raising the firing temperature or adding more flux, or try a different flux.

Calcining

Calcining is heating a raw ceramic material to between 800°C (1472°F) and 1000°C (1832°F), to remove any unwanted organic matter or moisture.

For example, if I wished to get rid of the carbon-trapping effect associated with horsetail, I could try calcining the raw ash at the bottom of the kiln in a biscuit firing to burn out the excess carbon. I use a previously biscuit-fired container kept for this process.

Miranda Forrest, bowls, 2007. All made from the one source
of clay on an English beach, fired unglazed to about cone 8 in
oxidation and reduction. Approximately 9 × 22 cm (3½ × 8½ in.).
Photo: by the author.

8

Found clay bodies

Native clay

This book is primarily about natural glazes and, as mentioned earlier, I have not found clay on the Outer Hebrides that is plastic enough to work with. Nevertheless, whenever I am on the mainland I keep an eye out for it. Some areas are more geologically inclined to have clay deposits than others. I check anywhere I can, where the subsoil is exposed, simply looking for sticky, clay-like material to test. So far I have only found clay deposits containing considerable amounts of iron; the contents of the clay you find will depend on the region. Clay is heavy to carry, so I tend to collect small amounts initially. About 1kg (2lb), will be enough to find out if it is worth collecting in larger amounts.

If you have found what you think is clay and want to try using it as a body, first test the plasticity by making a small pinch pot of some sort; mine usually resemble sleeping birds (see p. 79). If the clay performs well enough, you can try making a larger piece, but resist the temptation to fire it before you have fired the small pinch pot, as unknown clays can slump dramatically at higher temperatures. Fire the pinch pot in a saucer to see if it retains its shape at the temperature you want to fire it to.

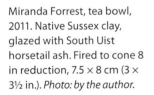

Miranda Forrest, tea bowl, 2011. Native Sussex clay, glazed with South Uist horsetail ash. Fired to cone 8 in reduction, 7.5 × 8 cm (3 × 3½ in.). *Photo: by the author.*

Cliffs of dry, powdery clay behind a Sussex beach, England.

BELOW: Pieces made with the thrown, unfired, native cliff clay shown above. The left-hand white pot is purchased white stoneware clay, for colour comparison. The right-hand small yellow pot is made from clay that was not very plastic, dug from a Sussex garden.
Photos: by the author.

I have collected clay on a pebbled English beach, found between high and low tidemarks. It proved to be surprisingly pure and did not require sieving. It was pale grey in colour and very plastic; I used it to throw the bowls illustrated on p. 72. Fired to cone 8, in reduction and oxidation, it produced varying shades of brown, indicating a higher iron content than I was expecting from the pale grey colour of the raw clay. I experimented with various glazes but preferred it unglazed. On returning some months later to collect more, I could not find any sign of it!

Another example of clay I found was a drier and more powdery form, with a 'yellow ochre' colour when wet. This sample was wetted to a slip and sieved to remove plant materials, then dried to the desired consistency on a plaster bat. It was found to be plastic enough to throw with and retained its shape when fired at cone 8. Examples of this clay are shown opposite, below and on pp. 73 and 78.

Clay stored in an airtight container will retain its consistency for some time. If all the organic matter has not been sieved out, it can rot, causing an unpleasant odour. Storing it somewhere cool helps prevent this. However, if more convenient, the clay can be dried for storage and re-soaked when required.

These examples are given to show how to assess native found clay. All these samples were vitrified and still retaining their shape at cone 8, but were just showing signs of overfiring, such as bloating, blistering or bubbling. Further experiments would involve lowering the top temperature to prevent this.

BELOW: Miranda Forrest, tea bowls, 2011. All native Sussex clay, fired to cone 8 in reduction. Rear: both sea-cliff-deposit clay, left glazed with South Uist horsetail ash, right with Sussex Japanese knotweed, 7.5 × 8 cm (3 × 3½ in.). Front: inland garden clay, glazed with South Uist horsetail ash, 4 × 5.5 cm (1½ × 2 in.). *Photo: by the author.*

Miranda Forrest, pendant,
2012. Raku-fired, incorporating
mica and iron ochre in the
glaze, 5 × 1.5 cm (2 × ½ in.).
Photo: by the author.

9 Natural materials for raku firing

Raku

The raku firing technique is well documented in other literature. Here I give examples of how I have incorporated found clay, mica and iron ochre into raku ware.

Raku firing temperature is typically 1000°C (1832°F). Consequently, found clays that slump or melt in higher firings can work well at raku temperatures. The tea bowl pictured on p. 78 is from the same source of clay as those on pp. 73 and 75, but has not begun to melt or blister in the same way. The glaze is a purchased alkaline raku glaze, but the iron from the clay body underneath has affected the colour during firing.

Mica is an alluring sparkly material found as small or large crystals; it is what glitters in granite rocks. It tends to be something one comes across while prospecting for glaze materials, rather than something one specifically goes looking for. Large crystals can sometimes be found embedded in rocks, like the one in the photo below.

It ranges in colour from silvery white (muscovite) to shiny black (biotite) and is sometimes golden. The larger crystals are structured as thin sheets that can be carefully separated with a knife blade. These sheets will remain as sheets at 1000°C (1832°F) but tend to melt and disappear above 1260°C (2300°F) – see pp. 54 and 55, nos. 29 and 30. When fired to 1000°C (1832°F) the silvery-white sheet crystals will become a strong gold colour. At raku temperatures, these sheets will not adhere to clay, but will adhere to glaze. Small crystals can be sprinkled onto glaze or mixed into it. Examples are show opposite and on p. 78.

Iron ochre can be used in varying amounts to colour a purchased raku glaze or the clay used for the body. When it is used to colour the clay body, it is likely to leach through into any glaze applied on top.

A golden-coloured mica crystal in a white feldspar/quartz rock. This crystal is about 4 cm (2 in.) across and will flake off in small sheet-like structures.
Photo: by the author.

ABOVE: Miranda Forrest, tea bowl, 2012. The native clay collected from cliffs and described in Chapter 8 (p. 74) was also used to make this tea bowl. The glaze is a purchased alkaline raku glaze, but it has become coloured during firing by iron in the clay, raku fired, 6.5 × 7.5 cm (2½ × 3 in.).

LEFT: Miranda Forrest, pendants, 2012. Raku-fired, incorporating mica and iron ochre in the glaze, from 3–5 cm (1¼–2 in.) high × 1.5–2 cm (½–¾ in.) wide.

OPPOSITE, TOP: Miranda Forrest, raku-fired bird, 2008. I have used varying coats of locally-dug hornblende mineral to give the darker colour on this piece. The white glaze is a purchased one, 15 cm (6 in.) high × 29 cm (11½ in.) long.

OPPOSITE BOTTOM: Miranda Forrest, sleeping bird memory catcher, 2011. Raku-fired, bird 10 cm (4 in.) long. I think there is room for fun and lightheartedness in my ceramics! Birds are abundant in my environment, and my 'pinch pots' tend to be birds. This one was made for experimenting with native clay slip and burnished with a beach pebble. The white is a purchased raku glaze. Sometimes I find a piece of driftwood is too interesting to be burnt, and shells can also be rather irresistible! They can all be incorporated into a piece that holds memories of a day out or seaside holiday.
Photos: by the author.

10

Ceramic artists working with natural materials

I thank the contributors to this chapter who very generously give an insight into the making of their work.

Fiona Byrne-Sutton

My large press-moulded vessels are physical, expressive of geological processes and electric-fired to 1160–1180°C (2120–2156°F) over 24 hours. These vessels, constructed from black earthstone, are embedded with clays I dig up near the principal rivers of Scotland. Iron oxide is also central to my work as the clays are usually saturated with iron oxide in one of its forms – black, ochre or red. These clays fire orange or deep brown so my work is a tale of orange and black, a colour combination with an ancient ceramic pedigree. However, within this there are big variations in vitrification temperature and also in the quantities of iron oxide present. It is not unusual to find iron-saturated clay marbled in alongside light-coloured clay. Some of the clays are very plastic and free of grit as in Clackmannanshire's high-firing Forth River and glacier boulder clay, which is marbled iron ochre and white before firing. Further downstream in Grangemouth, also on the Forth River, black iron oxide is the main mineral. The clay is much shorter, i.e. not very plastic, and it vitrifies to a glassy sheen around 1150°C (2102°F).

LEFT: Fiona Byrne-Sutton, *Clackmannanshire Slab Bowl* (detail), 2010. Clackmannanshire glacier boulder clay from Gartenkeir Farm, black earthstone, 55 × 19 cm (21½ × 7½ in.). *Photo: Michael Wolchover.*

RIGHT: Fiona Byrne-Sutton, *Clackmannanshire Glacier Boulder Clay Slip Bowl* (from above), 2012. Black earthstone, 55 × 19 cm (21½ × 7½ in.). *Photo: Amy Copeman.*

My bowls map out the geopoetics of place. They celebrate the Scottish land through each clay's properties, be it with coloured slips or by combining a low-vitrification clay with a higher-firing one. Thus in the *Grangemouth Forth River Bowl*, a very thick layer of unsieved leatherhard grey clay has been rolled into higher-maturing black earthstone and electric-fired at 1160°C (2120°F) over 24 hours. The melting Grangemouth clay has shrunk faster than the clay underneath, resulting in an attractive brown sheen and expressive cracks and fissures. The *Clackmannanshire Slab Bowl* is embedded with slabs of marbled clay from Gartenkeir Farm near Alloa. The *Clackmannanshire Forth River Bowl* features sieved slip from the same farm but dug higher up a slope. This is paler due to the preponderance of light clay over iron ochre at that point. Local flora is pressed in and painted over with red iron oxide, which fires to an attractive glassy grey sheen on black clay. These vessels, which have no obvious function, use the vocabulary of domestic ceramic craft – the bowl, the pouring cut in the lip, the rectangular handle incision in the vessel wall – to make statements about form and space.

I am attempting to develop an unsentimental craft that corresponds with the difficult times we live in, while not passing judgment. The bowls' round circle is an archetypal form. Measuring 55 cm (21½) across and 19 cm (7½) high, I intend my bowls to create an immense space for reflection. When the indigenous clays, and themes such as the plants and house motif come together on black, they set off a reverberation which pricks – a slight disturbance of consciousness which unsettles, asking questions of the viewer.

Fiona Byrne-Sutton, 2012

Fiona Byrne-Sutton, *Clackmannanshire Glacier Boulder Clay Slip Bowl* (in profile), 2012. Black earthstone, 55 × 19 cm (21½ × 7½ in.).

ABOVE: Fiona Byrne-Sutton,
*Grangemouth Forth
River Valley Bowl*, 2012.
Grangemouth clay, 55 × 19
cm (21½ × 7½ in.).

RIGHT: Fiona Byrne-Sutton,
*Grangemouth Forth River
Valley Bowl* (detail), 2012.
Grangemouth clay, 55 × 19
cm (21½ × 7½ in.).
Photos: Amy Copeman.

Louise Cook

Ever since my grandmother produced a bucket of clay from the shore of our family croft, I have had a love affair with clay. As children, my sister and I would sit and make simple shapes. I know now we were in fact making pinch pots. My memories of working with that strange lumpy material, with its earthy odour and the occasional small sea critter, are still strong. I just loved it!

After moving to the island of North Uist in Scotland's Outer Hebrides, I learned about peat/pit firing and began running workshops and clay days using local materials. After removing the still-glowing pot from the pit, I sprinkle it with milk and then plunge it into water. The milk provides interesting splatter patterns and appears, like a glaze, to be fairly permanent (p. 86, bottom). The resulting pinch pots appear very similar in colour and texture to many pottery shards being eroded from coastal archaeological sites throughout the Western Isles.

Being self-taught in ceramics has meant, at times, a steep learning curve to manage materials. I never shy away from putting organic materials into the kiln, but this has resulted in both great delights and occasional disasters. I began to collect sands and clay-like soil from Uist beaches and places I'd visit on holiday. I discovered that the local material on its own can't withstand the demands of a stoneware firing. I can, however, use it as a wash over prepared stoneware clay, and achieve rich dark browns with hints of metallic iron giving it a gunmetal finish (below). Used raw from the coast and bisque-fired, Uist material is terracotta in colour with an open gritty texture. There is a high percentage of mica, which produces a delicate sparkle even through the darker, peat-fired areas (below). Small grit chunks of quartz retain their brilliant white and provide an interesting contrast to the darker fired areas.

Louise Cook, mirrors, 2012. Shoreline-inspired impressions with a local wash and use of beach and loch sands as glaze. Fired to 1260°C (2300°F) in an electric kiln. Left: 17 × 8 cm (6¾ × 3¼ in.), right: 25.5 × 19.5 cm (10 × 7¾ in.). *Photo: by the author.*

ABOVE: Louise Cook, *Utah* wall panel, 2011. Stoneware fired to 1260°C (2300°F) in an electric kiln, 51 cm (20 in.). Individual tiles incorporating impressions from plant materials collected on walks across deserts in Utah and Arizona. Carved clay-stamp impressions are filled with clay-type soils from Utah, while a Uist wash gently highlights plant impressions.

RIGHT: *Utah* panel (detail). Individual tiles: 6 cm (2½ in.). *Photos: by the author.*

I feel my work is constantly evolving and the secret, I believe, is its simplicity. I now incorporate glazes made from beach sand and local clay materials. The sands generally produce honey/ochre/olive tones and sometimes a 'salt'n'pepper' finish (pp. 40 and 84, bottom). I have observed subtle differences among specific beaches along the west coast and delicate colour changes when the local slip is used as a base. I suspect this simplicity and my drive to experiment will keep me busy for years.

Louise Cook, 2012

Louise Cook, three-legged slab-rolled *Pebble Bowl* with seaweed impressions, 2003. Peat/pit-fired, 13 × 20 cm (5 × 8 in.). *Photo: by the author.*

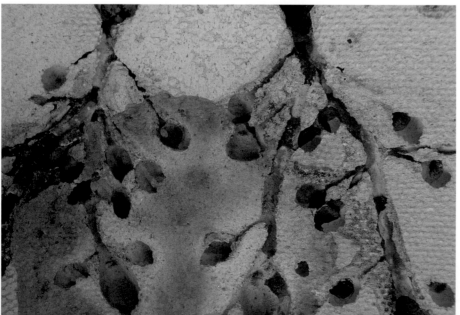

Louise Cook, slab-rolled *Pebble Bowl* with seaweed impressions (detail), 1999. Peat/pit-fired with milk glaze. In the collection of Lews Castle College. *Photo: by the author.*

Mike Dodd

For a long time now I have been using minerals for glaze-making that are usually, though not exclusively, in my vicinity: granites, hornfels, andesites, porphyries, clays, ochres and wood ashes. Check out local quarries. Many are mining and crushing rocks used for mixing with tarmac for road building and maintenance. Others are mining limestone and gypsum for the cement and plaster industries. Limestone/chalk, or whiting as we know it, is plentiful and cheap so I do not collect this. Gypsum is not recommended as a glaze material because of its sulphur content.

When you visit a quarry and see the manager or foreman, you need to ask for the dust fraction. Through the application of recent health and safety regulations this is now a 'wet dust fraction'. It is often fine enough that you can sieve out the larger pieces. If not, you have to crush it, requiring a plate mill and then a ball mill. Alternatively, ask if you can sweep up the dust in the screening sheds. These are the tall buildings that take the crushed rock by conveyor belt to the top and, through a series of sieves, grade the rock into different sizes. Lorries can then pull up underneath, open a hatch and fill their vehicles with the appropriate grade for their task. The dust in these sheds is fine and consistent (important for glazes). Some managers will allow you up into these sheds, armed with your plastic bags and a shovel, wearing a hard hat and accompanied by a member of staff; some managers won't let you near the site workings but may still provide you with bags of fine material. It's a good plan, at some later date, to present to the manager a pot or a few mugs glazed with some of the quarry's rock. These offerings are invariably well received.

Local clay is a lot easier to find, either in your garden or in the banks of a local river, or even on a building site where the digger is pulling out lovely green, grey, blue, red or yellow clay from the footings of a new build. Four or five bags of such clay – dried, slaked, sieved and dried again – will last for years as a glaze material. Wood ashes are, I think, self-explanatory!

Mike Dodd, 2012

Mike Dodd, local clay used in an ash glaze, 2011. High-fired stoneware, width: 22 cm (8¾ in.). *Photo: by kind permission of the Goldmark Gallery.*

Mike Dodd, basalt and granite black, 2011. High-fired stoneware, height: 23.5 cm (9¼ in.).

Mike Dodd, hornfels stone over clear feldspathic glaze with wax resist pattern, 2011. High-fired stoneware, height: 32 cm (12½ in.).

Mike Dodd, granite and
ash glaze over broken slip,
2011. High-fired stoneware,
height: 24.5 cm (9½ in.).

Mike Dodd, ash glaze over
garden clay slip, 2011.
High-fired stoneware,
height: 48.5 cm (19 in.).
*Photos: by kind permission of
the Goldmark Gallery.*

Lotte Glob

My creative process involves a close, continuing and intense relationship with the landscape and wilderness of the Scottish Highlands, a part of which is long hikes into the mountains, bringing back materials such as rocks and sediments. By working directly with these materials in a raw and unrefined state, combined with different clays, I create sculptural forms that are direct responses to the materials' physical nature. The sculptures are then fired to 1320°C (2408°F), white heat, undergoing physical alterations similar to those involved in the landscape's volcanic origins.

It is essential for me that the firing creates the conditions for the materials to become active again, thus reliving these metamorphoses. High risks are often taken during this process of melting rocks, glass, clay and sediment. Despite the knowledge I have developed through numerous experiments, the excitement of this process drives me to take calculated risks as I push these materials to an extreme where they will be irrevocably transformed.

I am a random potter; I don't work scientifically, but intuitively. I take lots of risks and have many surprises, both good and bad. I will try any natural materials I find. The materials I mostly use are black sand and white sand, and yellow and red earth I get from a riverbank. I use them mostly in the raw state, just as I bring it home; on plates and tiles, I layer them. Sometimes I mix it with wood ash or into my glazes or slip.

BELOW LEFT: Lotte Glob, *Just rocks*, 2005. Rock, 40 cm (15¾ in.) high.

BELOW RIGHT: Lotte Glob, *Magma lot* (detail), 2012. *Photos: Lotte Glob.*

I have always been interested in using materials for glazes found in a raw state in the land. I live in the northwest corner of Scotland, in a landscape famous for its geology, with lots of natural ingredients.

When I first started to use raw materials, I would grind them up meticulously. This was a lot of hard work, so I asked an old potter what would happen if I put a whole rock in the kiln. He threw up his hands in horror and said, 'No no, they will explode.' Next firing, I put a small rock in the kiln and it came out great – half-melted and no explosion. After that I put some more in the kiln and even bigger ones, too. I now use rocks regularly, at times just on their own, fusing them together. I try many different types: some melt completely, some come out beautifully and some hardly change.

Now I am much more aware of how a rock will perform in my kiln and I have a lot fewer disasters. Of course, there is always a new rock that I have not fired before, so I don't take things for granted. In that regard, I would not recommend anyone firing rocks unless they are prepared to take big risks (but, then, life is a risk). To protect my kiln shelves, I put a thick layer of silicate sand on the shelves before placing the ceramics on them. I have gone through a lot of kiln shelves over the years since I have been firing rocks.

Lotte Glob, 2012

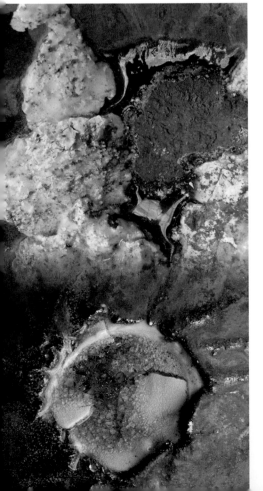

LEFT: Lotte Glob, 2006. High-fired stoneware, tile, earth, sand and glass (detail).

ABOVE: Lotte Glob, 2007. Boulder rocks, sand, mud and glass, 55 x 60 cm (21½ × 23½ in.). *Photos: Lotte Glob.*

Lotte Glob, plate, 2012. Rock, sediment and glass. High-fired stoneware, diameter: 60 cm (23½ in.). *Photo: Lotte Glob.*

Wendy Kershaw

I find ceramics a wonderful medium with which to create narrative illustrations; it is such a unique and infinitely variable surface to work with, a lifetime's worth of experimenting and play.

Sometimes in the past I have over-controlled the clay to the point where it has deadened the illustrations. It's a balancing act between control and letting things happen, imposing my will on the clay but letting it be itself. I have usually worked with a mix of underglaze stains, without glaze, firing to cone 6, where the stains bond enough with the clay so as not to rub off. Working with clay is like juggling lots of balls in the air – the type of clay, temperature, colourants, making method and decorating techniques. To experiment and keep things fresh I like to change one of those elements, and here I swapped my commercial underglaze stains for iron ochre, picked up in cold handfuls from the shore of a Scottish loch. Iron ochre can be spotted by its bright ruddy-orange colouring, usually found at the edge of a loch or where water is flowing.

At first I used the ochre in its raw state, after putting it through a 60-mesh sieve to get rid of the leaves and twigs, then through the finer 120-mesh. However, I found that using it raw led to the problem of crawling where it was laid down thickly. But it was easy to overcome this drawback by calcining the ochre, firing it above 800°C (1472°F) and thus getting rid of the excessive shrinkage. After calcining, I ground it down and mixed it with watered-down acrylic medium. The acrylic medium stops the ochre from powdering off when touched, making it easier to work into without the risk of smudging what is already there.

Wendy Kershaw, *Memory collecting the flowers mown down by time*, 2012. Porcelain, 27 cm × 30.5 × 0.5 cm (10½ × 12 × ¼ in.). *Photo: Wendy Kershaw.*

My technique involves drawing into leatherhard to dry slabs of clay with fine sewing needles, then biscuit-firing to cone 06. To give texture, I deliberately scuff the biscuited surface before flooding it with ochre, so that it runs into the incised lines. Then I rub off the excess with a soft cloth, which leaves a mid-tone. To lighten certain areas I apply a combination of washing over the whole surface with a dense makeup sponge, and cleaning smaller areas with a wet paintbrush. To bring up the white of the porcelain I use a pencil eraser and for very fine detail I use a scalpel. The darker tones are built up by painting on layers.

My illustrations are based on proverbs, sayings, and the celebration of domestic rituals. I try to create worlds where the often overlooked small joys of life can be more fully revelled in and some interesting quirks of human nature explored.

The Epic Bath (above) is a celebration of a long soak, a luxurious bath taken to extremes, with not only many bath salts, bubbles and a boat, but also involving large quantities of tea and cake. *Pudding girl in the bathroom cupboard* (opposite, bottom left and right) is a personal domestic myth, where the anticipation of longed-for pudding is expressed through the wearing of a many-pocketed dress, each pocket containing a pudding spoon ... just in case it is needed.

Wendy Kershaw, 2012

ABOVE: Wendy Kershaw, *The Epic Bath*, 2012. Porcelain, 42.5 × 46.5 × 0.5 cm (17 × 18 × ¼ in.).

OPPOSITE
TOP LEFT: Wendy Kershaw, *The Epic Bath* (detail), 2012.

RIGHT: Wendy Kershaw, *Pudding girl in the bathroom cupboard*, 2012. Porcelain, 39.5 × 13 × 0.8 cm (15½ × 5 × ¼ in.).

BOTTOM LEFT: Wendy Kershaw, *Pudding girl in the bathroom cupboard* (detail), 2012.

Photos: Wendy Kershaw.

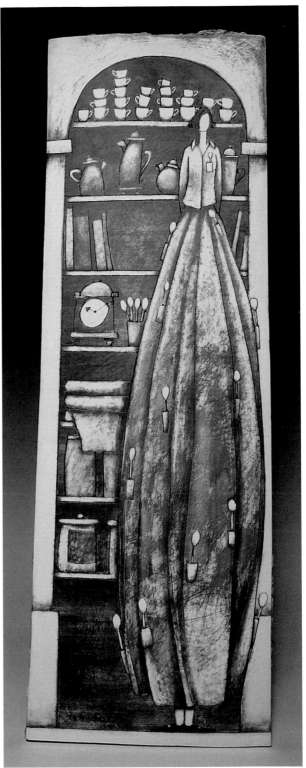

Phil Rogers

For as long as I have been making pots I have been interested in the notion that using materials found locally is a way to introduce a personal, if not unique, character into one's work. Making glazes, slips and even clay bodies in this way does not require a deep knowledge of chemistry. Far more important is an inquisitive mind and the desire to be more of a potter than those who rely on over-refined materials arriving neatly labelled in plastic bags from the supplier.

I live amidst a beautiful yet rugged landscape close to the source of the River Wye in Wales. Forestry is one local industry, and the unusable waste from the harvested wood supplies me with the fuel I need for one of my kilns and, from the fireboxes, the wood ash for my glazes. The wood-burning stove in my house and ash from the kiln provide me with all the ash that I need. Wood ash has been the central core of my glaze-making for 30 years and my work, particularly the surfaces of my pots, has developed very much to take advantage of the fluid, textured qualities of the ash glaze.

Glaze-making relies on silica. Silicon oxide is the main glass-forming oxide, and the task of the potter is to melt silica to form a glass or glaze. On its own, silica has a high melting point – quartz, for instance, melts at 1830ºC (3326ºF) – so we need to introduce to it what is known as an alkaline flux. Alkaline fluxes can be calcium, potassium, lithium, sodium or magnesium. Put simply, providing we mix one or more of these fluxes with silica in the correct proportion and in a fine-enough particle size, we can persuade the silica to melt at a much lower temperature that is within the scope of the potter's kiln. This is an example of the practice or theory of eutectics.

RIGHT: Phil Rogers, press-moulded bottle, 2012. Stoneware, height: 23 cm (9 in.). I coat the leatherhard pot with a red slip made from clay that I dig in the woods above the pottery. The clay is non-plastic and unsuitable for throwing but it makes a perfect iron-bearing slip. After biscuit firing I glaze the pot and, while the glaze is still wet, I drag my fingers across the surface, leaving a residual layer of glaze over the finger marks. The very thin layer of glaze is enough to flux the surface of the slip to this rich red colour which contrasts beautifully with the black tenmoku glaze.

FAR LEFT: Phil Rogers, *Yunomi*, 2012. Stoneware, hakeme with an incised pattern and an ash glaze, height: 12 cm (4¾ in.). I love the way ash glazes pool into hollows and on lines and ridges. I take advantage of this characteristic by carving through the thick slip into the clay body.

LEFT: Phil Rogers, *Chawan*, 2012. Stoneware, ash-glazed with an impressed pattern, height: 14 cm (5½ in.). The glaze on the lower portion of this bowl is made from wood ash mixed with a stone dust from a quarry near the Welsh border. The stone is known as greywacke, a degraded sandstone used in the road-construction industry. It is fairly high in iron and lends an olive colour to the glaze. *Photos: Phil Rogers.*

Near to my pottery is a quarry where the stone called greywacke is won. Greywacke is a very hard and durable impure sandstone used primarily in the road-surfacing industry. Known locally as gritstone, it is high in silica and contains approximately 4% iron. I collect the finest dust from the plant's extractor fans and use this material directly in some of my glazes (see bowl, right, on p. 96). The woods above the pottery are the source of a red clay that is non-plastic and totally unthrowable. However, it makes a wonderful underslip for my finger-wiped decoration (p. 97).

I have said that an extensive knowledge of chemistry isn't essential. In finding a new, potentially useful material, my routine is more intuitive than scientific and based on a 'see what happens' philosophy. If we are looking at glazes, my first step is to place a small button of the material in a glaze firing and see how much or how little it melts at my normal firing temperature of cone 11. The next step would be a line blend of two materials in combination. To a high-silica rock or a clay I might add a flux in the form of wood ash (wood ash is high in calcium) or possibly limestone (whiting). From the fired results of these mixtures, I would find the two or three most interesting combinations and then add a third material – possibly a clay or feldspar depending on what I think it needs – and fire another 10 mixtures. Often, we will have achieved a good glaze from these three materials and it can be as simple as that. A more detailed description of this process, together with more information about where to find suitable materials, can be found in my book *Ash Glazes*, published by A&C Black.

Utilising local materials is a way to produce glazes and surfaces that are truly your own. Even a basic understanding of geology and chemistry can reward you with quite amazing results. It is, in my opinion, part of the potter's role to understand the materials he or she uses and to form an intimate and prolonged relationship with them.

Phil Rogers, 2012

ABOVE LEFT: Phil Rogers, lidded caddy, 2012. Stoneware, height: 23 cm (9 in.). There are two ash glazes on this piece. The rim has an elm ash glaze and the lower portion a glaze made from a local quarry stone mixed with ash. I was given two large sacks of elm ash that had been lying in a garden shed for more than 30 years. The glaze has a beautiful, blue-grey colour unlike any other ash I have used.

ABOVE RIGHT: Phil Rogers, wood-fired jar, 2011. Stoneware, height: 28 cm (11 in.). I have used wood ash in the glaze on this piece. Almost all of the wood ash I use comes from the wood-burning stove in the living room of my house. I use waste wood from a local saw mill to fire the two-chamber wood kiln. *Photos: Phil Rogers.*

Joules Sargent

As a ceramic designer, I find the idea of producing work to a specific theme is not terribly hard. However, the production of a colour palette from natural, found and recycled materials, although labour-intensive, can be incredibly rewarding, with a myriad of wonderful results awaiting.

I live in an area that is formed of ancient deposits, both glacial and sedimentary. Consequently, the allure of using these in my work is undeniable. Luckily, I also have access to a great array of vegetation from which to choose, so collecting plants and test-firing have become a way of life.

As a flux, I use tall-stemmed summer flowers and plants high in silica, in the form of dry ash. I like to use mixed meadow flowers (meadow ash), borage, poppy and horsetails. For the glaze, I also use chalk that is dried, ground and mixed with the clay before firing.

The glacial clay I use is widespread throughout the south of England. This clay is yellow ochre before firing but turns a reddish tan at cone 8. I also use cliff-fall clay, which is stoneware. Colours range from black to red to pale purple due to its iron-oxide content, but all fire to an iron red. The final clay is an earthenware that will gloss if fired to cone 8, but it will also crawl, so needs other ingredients to keep it stable.

I find the inclusion of found and recycled materials to be rather exciting, too, as the results can be quite stunning. I use metals, glass, rock fragments and sand to add depth and texture. I fire mainly in oxidation but whatever the firing, I find the most exciting part is opening the kiln to reveal the glorious bounty nature has to offer, available on our doorstep if we wish to take up the challenge.

BELOW LEFT: Joules Sargent, small tea light, 2012. Porcelain top unglazed, base in stoneware with three glazes made from local clays, all using chalk as a flux. Base: 11.5 x 11.5 cm (4½ × 4½ in.), height of whole piece: 10 cm (4 in.).

BELOW RIGHT: Joules Sargent, ash-glaze tea light, 2012. Meadow ash and local earthenware glaze and borage with glacial clay glaze. Base: 11.5 x 11.5 cm (4½ × 4½ in.), height of whole piece: 12.5 cm (5 in.). *Photos: Joules Sargent.*

I have found these glazes complement the tea-light holders, giving them an extra lift in colour that is in contrast to their unglazed porcelain tops. These are embossed with floral patterns that allow for the transmission of light when lit. This is where I have found the delicate balance in nature between strength and fragility shining through in the final piece.

I have always had a love of astronomy, and making the moon bowls allows such freedom of expression for me. I add a lot of recycled materials to create unusual glazes with alternative surface decoration.

Joules Sargent, 2012

RIGHT: Joules Sargent, *Moon bowl 1*, 2012. Stoneware, clay and chalk glaze with cliff-fall clay and poppy glaze and recycled materials, diameter: 46 cm (18 in.).

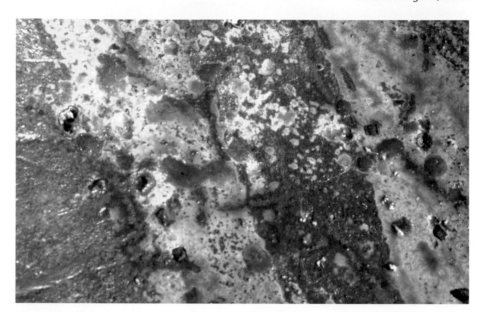

LEFT: Joules Sargent, *Moon bowl 1* (detail), 2012.

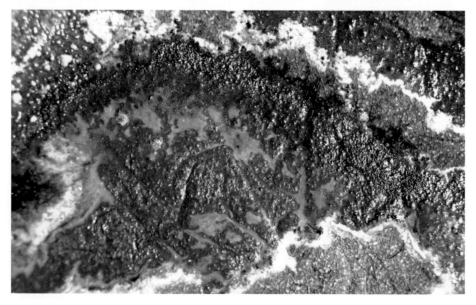

LEFT: Joules Sargent, *Moon Bowl 2* (detail), 2012. Stoneware, black sand with recycled glass pools with a mixed glaze centre.
Photos: Joules Sargent.

11

Gallery

Miranda Forrest, *The Mingulay Bowl*, 2010. Porcelain, fired to cone 9 in reduction, 11 × 27 cm (4½ × 10½ in.). *Photo: by the author.*

Mingulay is the penultimate island at the south end of the Outer Hebrides archipelago. It has a similar history to St Kilda 40 miles to the west, but unlike St Kilda, is now uninhabited.

Prior to a camping holiday on Mingulay, permission was obtained from the owners, the National Trust for Scotland, to collect small amounts of iron ochre (of which there is an abundance), dead grass, common reed stems and yellow flag iris leaves from the land, and cast-up seaweed from the beach. These ingredients, including an old bird's nest of grass found tumbling in the wind, were processed and used to glaze this bowl.

ABOVE: Miranda Forrest, wee dram pots, 2011. Porcelain, fired to cone 9 in reduction, 6 × 7 cm (2¼ × 2¾ in.). *Photo: by the author.*

I often use these 'wee dram', 'shot' or 'schnapps' pots for testing glazes. Ceramics are made for holding – the shapes the maker created passing into the hands of those who use them – it remains one of the intimate tactile arts. I love to change the shape of a thrown piece to give it interest and variety when held in the hand. Ceramics is also a visual art and I am continuously amazed by the range and appropriateness of colours in the glazes I make from natural materials.

RIGHT: Miranda Forrest, spiral lid pot, 2011. Stoneware, with glaze from mixed wet measurements of 2 parts potash feldspar (purchased), 1 part horsetail ash, 1 part iris ash (yellow flag), 1 part cereal straw ash. For comparison, see the wee dram pots above; the second from left (porcelain.) has the same glaze on it. Fired to cone 9 in reduction, 20 × 14 cm (8 × 5½ in.). *Photo: by the author.*

One of the intriguing aspects of making ceramics is that work often surprises its maker when they unpack the kiln. I think this applies even more when the materials used are natural, unrefined ones. This piece was one such case.

Miranda Forrest, pedestal bowl, 2011. Porcelain, fired to cone 9 in reduction, 7 × 12 cm (2½ × 4¾ in.). *Photo: by the author.*

This is one of my favourite glazes, made from reed and driftwood, from mixed wet measurements of 1 part potash feldspar (purchased), 1 part driftwood ash, 1 part reed ash, 8 × 13 cm (3 × 5½ in.). Other examples of this glaze can be seen on pp. 8, 66, 70 and 71. It subtly changes depending on thickness, firing temperature and, of course, the different driftwoods. The colour ranges from pale green to pale blue and is more intense where it pools.

Miranda Forrest, colours in a bowl reflected in the landscape, 2010. Porcelain, fired to cone 10 in reduction, 5 × 28 cm (2 × 11 in.). *Photo: by the author.*

This bowl is glazed with cereal straw, horsetail, nettle and a small amount of seaweed, brushed on and layered, all collected from the landscape in the photograph. I feel I have achieved the desire I had, when I first moved to South Uist, to bring the landscape literally as well as metaphorically into my ceramic work.

12

Health and safety

Marine vegetation

Historically, seaweeds have been collected worldwide for food, organic fertiliser and, of more relevance to us, for use in the glass and ceramics industry. Seaweed naturally contains arsenic in slightly higher amounts than most land vegetation. In this natural state, it's in the form of arsenic sugars, a relatively nontoxic form. However, when seaweed is burnt, the arsenic changes into a more toxic state that is released in the smoke. When it was collected and burnt in industrial quantities, this caused livestock and public-health problems.[1] Even when burning small amounts, you should take care to note which direction the smoke is moving so that it is not inhaled. Moreover, kilns in which seaweed ash is fired should have a flue. **Ceramicists often experiment with seaweed because of its reputation as a known natural glaze maker but they should also be aware of the small quantities of arsenic it contains and take sensible precautions when processing it.**

Collecting materials

Materials for natural glazes are often found where the land is unstable. Be aware of this and take sensible precautions such as wearing the correct footwear; wearing a hard hat (for sale in DIY stores) if anything is likely to fall from above; and informing someone else where you are going or taking someone with you. Always ask permission before collecting materials or going onto private land.

I try to collect rocks that do not need fragmenting, but if you're breaking up rocks with a hammer, *always* wear thick gloves and goggles to protect your eyes. Wear other protective clothing too, as fragments of rock can be very sharp, and be aware of other people around you.

Wear any necessary protective clothing when collecting plants, such as gloves for nettles or thistles, or if you have any known allergy to certain plants. Some have surprisingly sharp stems where they have snapped off, so be careful when bending down that stems do not stab you, in particular your eyes.

Miranda Forrest, vase with flowers, 2011. Porcelain, with glaze from mixed wet measurements of 1 part 'cone 8' base glaze, 1 part wild angelica ash. Fired to cone 9 in reduction, 9 × 7 cm (3½ × 3 in.). This vase is constructed with an internal ring to facilitate easier flower arranging. *Photo: by the author.*

[1] Reference material: G. J. Riekie, P. N. Williams, A. Raab, A. A. Meharg 2006, *The potential of kelp manufacture to lead to arsenic pollution of remote Scottish Islands*, Aberdeen University.

Burning materials

Before lighting a fire, check that the site is clear of obstacles and have a fire extinguisher to hand. Any smoke is toxic so do not inhale it. Also be mindful that other people are not in the direct path of the smoke. Be aware of the possibility of airborne sparks igniting dry vegetation downwind. **Do not leave a fire unattended.**

Caustic materials

Do not inhale dry ashes; always wear a mask when disturbing them. Ashes are caustic so avoid getting them on your skin and always wear gloves when handling them. Wear latex or similar waterproof gloves when working with all glaze slops.

Clay is only a health problem if inhaled as a dust. Do not inhale any ceramic dust. Always clean up in the studio with a wet sponge or mop, *never* a dry brush.

Kiln firing

Do not fire unknown substances in a kiln without a flue. This is particularly relevant in an unventilated studio or one without an extractor system. Always assume toxic fumes may be released during firing. Follow the manufacturer's instructions for firing the kiln.

General

Be mindful that natural materials may contain toxic substances. 'Natural', in the context of this book, includes unrefined and untested. Enquire locally as to whether there are unusually high concentrations of potentially toxic materials present, as this is usually something that is generally known about. Government bodies, universities and environmental agencies are sources of such information.

Food safety

Many countries have legislation that applies specifically to ceramics intended for serving food. Information on legislation for the UK is held by the National Archives (www.legislation.gov.uk/all?title=ceramics), and other countries will have applicable information available. Make yourself aware of these rules and restrictions if it applies to your work.

I have had final glaze results from the materials in this book tested and they passed the current legislation that applies for serving food on ceramics in the United Kingdom. There are many labs that will test materials for you, but I used Ceram Research Ltd, Queen's Road, Penkhull, Stoke-on-Trent, Staffordshire, ST4 7LQ (www.ceram.com).

Conclusion

As a general rule most people who make ceramics have a penchant for a certain part of the process, whether it is a particular aspect of making, glazing or firing. I never really enjoyed the glazing stage until I began using collected materials. It now flows more naturally for me and I like the link my work has with my local environment.

Glaze materials I collect make connections with other aspects of my life. As a hobby I keep a small flock of native Hebridean sheep and hand-spin and knit their fleeces. When asked to make a felted hat for an exhibition at a native-breed sheep conference, I added a raku-fired ceramic detail with an iron ochre in the glaze that I found in the field where my sheep live (see below).

I find much satisfaction and fascination in my work with natural glazes and I hope that you find using natural materials equally as enthralling. Go for a walk and see what you can find! Some iron ochre? Paint it under or over a base glaze and it will not only give the piece of work an identity, but will become part of the narrative of your walk – or is it your walk that becomes part of the narrative of the pot?

Miranda Forrest, hand-spun, knitted and felted hat, 2012. Raku-fired ceramic detail with found iron-ochre decoration. *Photo: by the author.*

Bibliography

Angus, Stewart, *The Outer Hebrides: The Shaping of the Islands* (Cambridge: The White Horse Press, 1998).

Cardew, Michael, *Pioneer Pottery* (London: A&C Black, 2002).

Daly, Greg, *Glazes and Glazing Techniques* (London: A&C Black, 2003).

Dassow, Sumi von, *Low-firing and Burnishing* (London: A&C Black, 2009).

Dodd, Mike, *An Autobiography of Sorts*, (Hampshire: Canterton Books, 2004).

Ellis, Clarence, *The Pebbles on the Beach* (London: Faber and Faber, 1972).

Leach, Bernard, *A Potter's Book* (London: Faber and Faber, 1976).

Mathieson, John, *Raku* (London: A&C Black, 2002).

Obstler, Mimi, *Out of the Earth, into the Fire* (Ohio: The American Ceramic Society, 2000).

Rhodes, Daniel, *Stoneware and Porcelain* (London: Sir Isaac Pitman and Sons Ltd, 1969).

Rogers, Phil, *Ash Glazes* (London: A&C Black, 2003).

Rothery, David, *Teach Yourself Geology* (London: Hodder & Stoughton Ltd, 2003).

Sutherland, Brian, *Glazes from Natural Sources* (London: A&C Black, 2005).

Miranda Forrest, small vase, 2011. Porcelain, poured glaze from mixed wet measures of 1 part Cornish stone (purchased), 1 part horsetail ash, 1 part iris ash (yellow flag), 1 part cereal straw ash. Fired to cone 8 in reduction, 4.5 × 6.5 cm (1¾ × 2½ in.). *Photo: by the author.*

Index